SACRIFICE AND
THE DEATH OF CHRIST

M. G. Totchen

ST. HUGH'S

1978

Centre for
Faith and Spirituality
Loughborough University

SACRIFICE AND THE DEATH OF CHRIST

Frances M. Young

Foreword by
Maurice Wiles

LONDON
SPCK

First published 1975
by the SPCK
Holy Trinity Church
Marylebone Road
London NW1 4DU

Printed in Great Britain by
Northumberland Press Limited
Gateshead

SBN 281 02845 1

Contents

Acknowledgements

Thanks are due to the following for permission to quote from copyright sources:

Bruno Cassirer (Publishers) Ltd and Simon and Schuster Inc.: *Christ Recrucified (The Greek Passion)* by Nikos Kazantzakis

Cambridge University Press: Origen *Contra Celsum*, tr. H. Chadwick, © 1965 by Cambridge University Press

Foreword

How can the ordinary Christian today make sense of ideas that come from the very different world of Greece or Palestine some two thousand years ago? How also can he assimilate the very technical work of theological scholarship in his own day? These are two very real problems of communication of which the thoughtful Christian is acutely aware. This book makes a valuable contribution to both of them.

'Sacrifice' is a concept deeply embedded in the ancient world. To understand its significance in Christian thought and worship calls for detailed scholarly work. Dr Young wears her scholarship lightly but it is a very thorough knowledge of the meaning of sacrifice in the ancient world on which she draws. But it is not enough simply to be provided with scholarly knowledge about sacrifice in the ancient world in a readable form. We need also to consider what role, if any, such ideas can be expected to play in the life of the Church today, what equivalents they may have in our contemporary society. The book seeks to probe this further theme also. Few books that I know deal with either of these themes as carefully or as sensitively in so short a compass—let alone both. I am very happy to recommend it as the kind of book that is so often asked for and so seldom written.

MAURICE WILES

To
A.T.

Author's Preface

This brief study has developed out of five lectures delivered in spring 1971, when the clergy of St Martin's-in-the-Bull-Ring, Birmingham, invited me to contribute to their programme for the general public, an invitation for which I am most grateful. It seemed an admirable opportunity for presenting the conclusions I had reached after several years' work for the degree of Doctor of Philosophy (University of Cambridge). The dissertation, entitled 'The Use of Sacrificial Ideas in Greek Christian Writers from the New Testament to John Chrysostom', contains the detailed evidence and discussions on which Part I of the present volume is based; this more scholarly version is to be published by the Philadelphia Patristic Foundation at a later date. Meanwhile, it seemed worthwhile to offer some of the conclusions to a wider public, especially since the occasion for reframing the principal ideas in a briefer and less academic form had been provided by the St Martin's lectures. The interest stimulated there encourages me to hope that others will find the following discussion helpful and suggestive. More interpretative material has been added in the present version.

I wish to acknowledge my debt to the supervisors of my research, Dr R. M. Grant of the University of Chicago, and Professor Maurice Wiles, whose continuing encouragement and friendship I greatly value. Without their suggestions and criticisms, my work would have been much impoverished. To these must be added my colleague, Michael Wilson, who in informal discussion has contributed much to the material in Chapter 6, all of which falls outside my specialist field. Any mistakes and errors in judgement are entirely my responsibility and would have been more numerous without the kind assistance of those mentioned. Thanks are also due to my father, who not only set my feet on an academic path, but gave valuable hours to the preparation of the index for this volume.

INTRODUCTION

Why discuss sacrifice?

Why discuss sacrifice?

Why discuss sacrifice? A good question, it may be felt. Sacrificial images are hardly those which arrest the attention of most people today. It might well seem that the subject of this book is irrelevant in the context of modern culture and the twentieth-century Church. Sacrifice does not appear at first sight to be a potential 'growth-point' for interpreting the gospel now. It conjures up memories of warm appeals to wash in the blood of the Lamb or cold requirements to give up meat for Lent. Indeed for some of the more radical theologians old-fashioned ideas like sacrifice are not merely irrelevant, but part of a religious system that must be rejected, along with anything else that smells of outmoded ritualism or religiosity. The love and brotherhood of Christ must be set free from the distortions of 'religion' and be rediscovered in the midst of secular society, they say. For such thinkers, sacrifice is too closely linked with conventional images of God as a supernatural figure who is just, demanding, and loving by turns, a figure that is 'dead' in the modern world.

Such an attitude is understandable, but it has unfortunate consequences. By deliberately enlarging the gulf between contemporary expressions of Christianity and the traditional language of the Scriptures and the Church, it makes it more difficult for the average churchgoer to understand the religious language he uses in worship; it makes it almost impossible for him to see the continuity of his responses and religious experiences with those of Christians of the past. This is a high price to pay while still in fact failing to make intelligible contact with non-churchgoers. To shout the irrelevance of religion and the death of God does nothing to make Christ relevant to this generation, and ignores the fundamental religious impulses of human beings (indeed, sociologists tell us that the majority of people confess to believing in God, and many still pray in difficulties, even though most no longer participate in church activities). Besides, this radical rejection of the past and concentration on worries about whether traditional notions of God are still credible has obscured the fundamentally distinctive and characteristic claim of Christianity, the real gospel of the Church, which is a gospel of salvation and redemption. Of course, this aspect is never entirely absent from the discussion, and theological expositions inevitably betray, consciously or unconsciously, a certain understanding of what salvation in Christ means. Indeed, concern with this point is revealed in the fact that the World Council of Churches has undertaken a wide-ranging discussion of the subject 'Salvation today'. Yet it is so easy to put the cart before the horse, to 'theologize' without first articulating the experience which gave it initial impetus, to criticize without acknowledging the value of what one has inherited. The standard works on the history of atonement doctrine and the meaning of sacrifice all date from the early years of this century; yet new historical insights and changes in theological thinking would make a considerable difference to any modern work of that kind. Do we not need to consider again the classic expositions of what salvation and atonement mean, before we have any hope of translating the gospel into relevant contemporary categories? This is not to underestimate the recent work of F. R. Barry and F. W. Dillistone,[1] but rather to stress the importance of more debate and discussion in this area. Christianity surely stands or falls in the last analysis on its gospel of redemption, and we cannot ignore the need to give that gospel rational expression as the basis for theological definition.

4

Historically speaking, it is in fact the case that response and experience preceded attempts to articulate and explain; christological categories and theological definitions were subsequent upon profoundly felt reactions to Jesus Christ within a particular cultural context. The classic example is perhaps that of Athanasius, the fourth-century bishop of Alexandria. His *De Incarnatione* could be described as the first attempt to expound the doctrine of atonement. In the history of doctrine, however, Athanasius is chiefly remembered for having forced the Church to make an unequivocal statement about the divinity of Jesus Christ. He did this precisely because of his understanding of what salvation in Christ meant, and argued his christological position from the natural presuppositions induced by his sense of Christ's saving work. For him, Jesus Christ had released frail mankind from ignorance, sinfulness, and mortality, and endowed it with the principle of God's life and perfection; therefore, Athanasius argued, he must have been the fullness of God in man. This argument presupposes an underlying experience of release from bondage, followed by an articulation of that experience in terms of what seemed, in that particular cultural situation, the most oppressive of human weaknesses. In other words, the experience of redemption and its expression were primary, theological conclusions only secondary.

We can in fact discern the same process in contemporary theology. One cannot help wanting to ask modern radical theologians why they should bother with theology at all. Why not just go to the logical extreme and abandon it altogether, along with the Church and the paraphernalia of Christianity? What is the point of 're-expressing' in a way that leaves little distinctive role for theology at all? The answer of course is that, for them, there is *something* in it. Through the medium of Christian theology—indeed, whether they like it or not, ultimately through the institutions of the Church—they have found something of such value that they cannot merely discard it. Nor is this simply a fear of losing their jobs and livelihood. Their verbal contortions and paradoxical utterances about waiting on a God who is dead,[2] and celebrating the death of God as an epiphany of the eschatological Christ, present in the fullness of the history before us, betray their reluctance to abandon something that gives hope, value, and meaning to their lives. They are trying to preserve in contemporary language the 'redemption' they have sensed in the creaking ecclesiastical structures and the outmoded language of Christianity. The image of Christ informs their faith and their ethics. Of course, there is also a strong element of reaction against the past; there is passionate impatience with the vehicle of the message. But there is some response to its content. They may assert that modern man has come of age, is religionless, that an end has come to any system of thought or action in which God or gods serve as a fulfiller of needs or solver of problems. But they recognize in Christ a way of responding to the darkness of suffering and the enigmas of human existence, a way of finding true liberation. They may refuse to accept a 'God-shaped blank' within man, but they assume the need for an ethic and a freedom which is Christ-shaped. Indeed, their very rejection of God is partly a recognition of the damage done to the liberating force of Christ by the fact that he has been institutionalized and dogmatized. Thus, even in this radical case, my point holds: response to the gospel of redemption is primary, and expositions of this in theological terms are secondary.

In fact the New Testament itself is one of the clearest witnesses to this sequence of development. Christological ideas developed because of the experience of salvation in Christ. The New Testament was produced by various people in various circumstances to meet the various needs of the Christian community. The New Testament is not *a* book but many books, and the different authors present us with theologies which are in various ways different from one another. Indeed, by the methods of form criticism, it is possible to see different view-points preserved alongside one another in a single Gospel. The New Testament is not homogeneous in its ideas; it bears the marks of its time and is written from several contemporary religious and philosophical standpoints. Nevertheless, underlying its variety of expression, there is a common experience of redemption, a fact which illustrates the primacy of the sense of salvation over subsequent 'theologizing'. The early Christians were searching for categories, for means of stating their beliefs about the person who was at the centre of their experience. No single category was adequate. In the early Christian writings we find a multiplicity of titles and ideas drawn from the available cultural background, differently emphasized, variously used, but producing in combination a radically new type of claim about this person, a claim that was intimately linked to the experience of him as the solution to their needs and concerns. What has the Synoptic message concerning the coming of the kingdom in common with Paul's elaborate metaphor of justification or with the transformed Gnosticism of the Johannine literature? The answer lies in the fact that all these different ways of expressing it reflect a common experience, a common reaction to Jesus, a reaction which demands extraordinary expression and for which no single type of approach was adequate. The fundamental reality is the effect of Jesus on a wide range of characters whose association together under any other circumstances would appear improbable. The Hellenizer and the Rabbi, the conservative and the liberal, the priest and the nationalist, the fisherman and the Pharisee, the Jew and ultimately the Gentile also, apparently experienced something which each could express in his own terms as being ultimate. Thus, for the early Palestinian community, steeped in the hopes and imagery of Jewish apocalyptic and messianic expectation, to understand Jesus as Son of Man or Messiah was meaningful; it was relevant to their deepest needs and concerns; such titles expressed their sense of fulfilment in him, however much he had disappointed their preconceived ideas of the Coming One. For the Gentile churches, a more meaningful understanding was found in the title 'Lord'; it expressed for them his unique status and authority over their lives, compared with all other authorities, political or religious. For Paul, obsessed with the claims of the Jewish law, Jesus Christ was above all the fulfilment and end of all moral endeavour, the solution to moral incapacity. For the writer to the Hebrews, the title which made Christ existentially relevant was 'High Priest'; it was because he answered the search for a ritual solution to sin and guilt, the need for mediation with a holy God—indeed answered it so superlatively as to render any other solution utterly inadequate. To the more philosophically inclined author of John's Gospel, he was the Logos of God, the ground and purpose of the universe, the light which overcame the darkness of the world, and the Way, the Truth, and the Life for the believer; in him the solution of the gnostic quest was given gratis to those who responded. We could enumerate further examples, but this will suffice to make the point. It was only because they could say, 'He means this to me' that they went on to say, 'He must be so-and-so'. The remarkable thing is that so many different people all said essentially the same thing: that he was the solution to their deepest needs and concerns. The multiplicity of ideas and theologies is a testimony to the extraordinary effect of the events surrounding this man, Jesus of Nazareth.

Ultimately this is the heart of the matter. This is what Christianity is all about. The expression of the experience, the proclamation of this gospel, is the central matter of Christian concern.

Now if this is so, it is clear that the perennial question concerns this redemption: how is the experience to be articulated in a way that makes it relevant to the ultimate concerns of contemporary mankind? But if this is our task, why embark upon it by discussing such an obviously irrelevant idea as sacrifice?

The question is natural enough, but is it not short-sighted? We have seen that the characteristically Christian claims developed because of the articulation of an experience of salvation within various cultural contexts. This articulation led to many different ways of expression, but because of the cultural environment, sacrifice was by far the most important of the images used. Christianity was born into an age and culture saturated with religion, and if it is true to say that there is hardly a religion of man which has not involved the practice of sacrifice, this general statement is even more applicable to the period and culture in which Christianity grew up. The offering of sacrifice was a universal rite in all the religions of the ancient world. The various tribes and nations which made up the Roman Empire all had traditional cults, in all of which sacrifice played a central part. It was not merely the practice of less civilized people, like the tribes of North Africa, Spain, Gaul (France), and Britain; it was the normal mode of worship in the sophisticated culture of the Jews, the Greeks, the Egyptians, and the Romans up to the time when the Emperor Constantine was converted to Christianity.

So in the world in which Christianity developed, sacrifice was assumed, and it is hardly surprising that the early Church had to work out its attitude towards it. In speaking of the early Church, we refer not merely to the New Testament period, but to the first three or four centuries during which Christian ideas were developing. The distinctive thing about Christians in that period was that they refused to sacrifice; and because of this, the general world outside despised and hated them for their 'atheism' —a somewhat surprising taunt in this day and age! Their refusal to sacrifice also exposed them to persecution. From time to time the Emperor issued decrees, requiring a token act of sacrifice as an expression of political loyalty (rather like saluting the flag); but Christians would not compromise. They preferred condemnation and death. For obedience to the decree implied recognition and worship of gods that they regarded as idols or evil demons. They were atheists to this extent, that they refused to believe in or worship the traditional gods.

Christians did not use sacrifice as the means of worshipping their own God, either. But on the other hand, they did inevitably use the vocabulary connected with sacrifice to describe their own acts of worship. For sacrifice was the only way of worship known, and so, even though they no longer practised it literally, the Christians spoke of their worship as the offering of spiritual sacrifices. The result is that sacrificial language is embedded in the liturgies used by all the major Christian denominations, and, even in churches with less formal liturgical patterns, sacrifice is never far from the lips of the preacher or evangelist. The most important reason for this is the fact that the New Testament uses the idea of sacrifice to explain the death of Christ. So scriptural expression of the Christian gospel of salvation is saturated with sacrificial terminology. We hear of 'atonement through the blood of Christ', language that comes direct from ancient sacrificial rites. In fact, no treatment of the death of Christ escapes from using words and phrases which originated in the practice of sacrificing animals. We find such phrases in hymns and prayers, books of devotion, and the liturgies of baptism and eucharist. So even though Christians rejected sacrifice, the idea is engrained in Christian tradition and Christian language.

Today we live in a culture in which the practice of sacrifice is totally foreign—no doubt largely because of the influence of Christianity down the centuries. But the result is that we no longer seem to be in a position to know *instinctively* what the sacrifice language of our traditions really means. In fact, we get certain preconceptions about the meaning of sacrifice and so misinterpret the real point of the language we are using. Many books on the subject expound theories of sacrifice which are in fact modern reconstructions with little evidential basis in the ancient texts. The most common misconception when sacrifice language is applied to the death of Christ runs something like this: 'God was angry with sinners. The Jews had tried to placate his anger by symbolically offering the lives of animals to him in place of their guilty selves. But this was inadequate and so Jesus offered a perfect sacrifice. He died as our substitute to appease God's anger.' With certain degrees of sophistication, this is the general picture one gets from listening to sermons or reading the majority of easily available books. Yet it is far from doing justice to the real religious outlook of the Jews, or the early Christians who used sacrificial terminology to sense the depth of meaning in the death of Christ. Clearly, if we are going to be able to appreciate the language of the liturgy and the New Testament, of our hymns and prayers, we need to go back and try to understand what sacrifice meant in the ancient world and what the new use of sacrifice language in Christianity meant to the worshippers of that time.

One reason, then, why it is short-sighted to suggest that sacrifice is irrelevant, is the fact that Christian expression is mediated to us through the traditional language of the Church, which is saturated with sacrificial imagery. Of all the images employed this was the most relevant and the most comprehensive used in the formative years of Christianity. Misunderstanding of this imagery has impoverished and narrowed the Church's thinking about both the cross and the eucharist, and to open up again a wider perspective on the subject could enhance mutual understanding among Christians of different traditions. To clear away misunderstanding, to rediscover the original meaning of the sacrificial language of the Church, is one aim of this book.

To investigate the subject fairly we have to develop a degree of sympathy with people living in a very different atmosphere. It is no good simply transferring our conceptions and definitions to their language and presuppositions. For us, the phrase 'to make a sacrifice' means to give up something that we value. The used car dealer advertises 'Bargains, Sacrifices', claiming that he is giving up some of the profit margin he might have expected. If a woman sacrifices the best years of her life to caring for aged parents, she gives up opportunities which she might have enjoyed. The S.C.M. Press Lent book for 1966 was entitled *Is sacrifice outmoded?* The author, Kenneth Slack, presented a very valuable argument to the effect that there is still a place for creative sacrifice in modern life, for giving up personal gains and pleasures in order to better society, to help afflicted individuals or unite the Church. The book illustrates modern usage. But connotations change in different cultures. The word originally implied 'to make an offering to a god' or 'to sanctify'. If we are to appreciate the meaning of sacrifice in religion generally and in Christianity in particular, we need to forget our idiomatic use and return to the original idea. Sacrifice comes from cults, from rituals of worship, from the sacred religious practices of mankind. In fact, sacrifice is integral to the religious response to the universe. The fact that it is necessary to stress this shows how far the modern world has moved from understanding and appreciating the intentions of sacrifice.

To ensure the prosperity of British Leyland by slaughtering bulls and goats with solemn ritual is simply not on.

But even today, away from the cushioning of modern developed society, in parts of the world where people still live close to primitive traditions and react instinctively to the wonders and disasters of the natural world with awe and fear, sacrificial rites are practised. And for us, two modern novels provide insight into this mentality, showing graphically how instinctive these reactions are where the 'cushioning' is removed.

The first example offered is John Steinbeck's *To a God Unknown*.[3] This is the story of a young man who leaves his Vermont home to 'homestead' in California. He has a deep emotional response to the land, a passion which amounts to sexual involvement. Steinbeck portrays the primitive instincts of man in response to the fertility of the land, his cattle, his wife. Two points are particularly relevant to our exploration of sacrifice.

1. Soon after his arrival, Joseph gets a letter telling him of his father's death and at that moment, in some instinctive way, he knows that his father's spirit has come to rest in a great tree under which he is building his ranch. As the novel proceeds, his involvement with and dependence on the tree become more and more apparent. He seeks the tree's approval of his bride, he pours wine over its roots, he hides portions of meat in its branches—a sacrificial religion is developing before our eyes, as an instinctive response to the tree and what it embodies. Conflict develops with his brother, a devout Protestant who senses the implications of his brother's action. This conflict comes to a head when Joseph wants to put his new-born baby into the tree's branches, another instinctive reaction exactly parallel to the offering of first-born found, for example, in the Old Testament. The brother leaves. Soon afterwards the tree is

found dying, destroyed by the brother before he departed. But when life has gone from the tree, life goes out of Joseph and out of his land: the dreadful dry years come.

2. As the novel proceeds, Joseph becomes more and more identified with the dying land. He remains when everyone else leaves, seeking water. He remains in the desert, struggling to keep water flowing in a sacred spring among the pines, the symbol that the land might still have life deep down. Finally the spring dries up, and instinctively Joseph tries to restart it by sacrificing a calf and draining the blood into it. But that is not sufficient; again by force of instinct he lies on the rock and slashes his own wrists to drain the blood into the dead spring. As he dies, the rains begin. He sacrifices his life for the life of the land; he knows in his bones that the blood is the life, that blood offered in sacrifice can give back life to the dying land. We shall find the expression of this belief in the Old Testament, where the blood is interpreted as the life.

There is in fact a lot more to the novel than this. There is portrayed an underlying conflict between Protestantism, Catholicism, and the 'nature-religion' practised by Joseph and one or two others. There is a subtle parallel drawn between Joseph and Jesus. There is much that sheds allusive light on the Christian belief in atonement through the blood of Christ. But at this point I merely want to stress that here we can experience in some measure the deep emotional response to life which produces the sacrificial practices of mankind.

The other novel to which I wish to draw attention is William Golding's Lord of the Flies,[4] the well-known account of a group of schoolboys aged between five and twelve, who crash-land on an idyllic coral island with no surviving grown-ups. At first, everything is marvellous fun, but then fears and terrors seize them, fears of unknown beasts lurking in the forests, or coming out of the sea, or appearing on the mountain. This overshadows the group as conflicts develop between the two leaders and gradually the thin veneer of 'civilization' is lost. The boys cover their innocence with war-paint and lose their shame. They appease the 'beasts' of their imagination with sacrificial offerings. They banish their fears in frenzied ritual dances, and as they lose consciousness of what they are doing, one of the boys is ritually murdered. The conflict becomes tribal warfare. Another boy is killed. The book ends with a vindictive hunt for the deposed chief. Death hangs over his head, when a ship arrives to rescue them and the captain laughs at their 'games' and their 'war-paint'. The 'Lord of the Flies' is the head of a pig which they had hunted and killed for meat. They stuck the head on a stick as an offering to the fearful beast. But the beast is only imaginary—the real enemy is within; the beast is in the nature of those well-brought-up little boys and it leads them to passion and murder and horrors they could hardly take in, even when they had committed them. The situation is depicted as bringing out the worst in human nature, even the tyranny and cruelty of a Hitler, and the treachery of friends under torture.

Are these two novels foreign to our time? They were written in this century in the developed societies of Britain and the U.S.A., but they depict instincts and attitudes which we think we have outgrown. Or have we? Do they not strike a chord of recognition? In spite of every appearance to the contrary, we can in the dress of these novels share in the instinctive response to the human condition and its environment which finds its expression in the act of sacrifice. They may enable us to enter more sympathetically into the culture of the ancient world in which Christianity was formed.

But they may do more than this. They may help us to

rediscover certain basic human responses and reactions. Novelists can utilize sacrificial practices because, in the course of this century, anthropologists and psychologists have recognized the importance of myths and rituals as a means of dealing with fundamental human drives, needs, and problems. We may not expect sacrifice to meet an immediate response in the modern cultural setting, but men still seem to need substitutes for it if they are to accept and come to terms with their suppressed drives and emotions. We shall explore this further in a later chapter. Here let us just hazard the suggestion that there is a large gap in modern culture, partially filled by music and drama no doubt, but still a void, unrecognized and unfilled because the Church is too apologetic and defensive about its claims, and too much bound to traditional and cramping expositions of the saving gospel it has to proclaim. The trouble is that familiarity breeds contempt, and narrow expositions of the sacrifice of Christ in terms of conservative theology no longer strike a chord in most people today. Perhaps if we can rediscover the vital meaning of sacrifice and why it seemed relevant to our predecessors, we might be half-way to understanding the needs of our contemporaries and discovering, as the early Christians did, that Jesus Christ answers to their ultimate needs, concerns, and values.

So, to the question why discuss sacrifice, two replies may be advanced: (i) because misunderstanding of the idea has impoverished our use of the traditional imagery through which Christian experience has been mediated to us, and (ii) because sacrifice once expressed a range of basic human reactions which are still part of our own psychological make-up, and an insight into these may help us to appreciate afresh the saving relevance of the Christian gospel.

The task before us then is clear. In the first place we need to re-examine the original cultural setting in which Christianity developed in order to discover again the sort of meanings and connotations that sacrifice then had; then we need to ask what are the implications of this historical study for the life of the modern Church and for contemporary witness to the saving power of the gospel.

PART I

Sacrifice in early Christianity

I

Different types of sacrifice

In the ancient world, as we have already noted, the practice of sacrifice was universal. For this reason it was taken for granted. So, in literature spanning one thousand years or so, we find no attempts to define sacrifice. It never occurred to anyone that it needed explanation or definition. The first definition in fact occurs in the writings of a Christian theologian in the dying days of the Roman Empire,[1] when Christianity itself had made sure that literal sacrifice was a thing of the past.

Sacrifice, then, was assumed. Its meaning was not defined. People just instinctively used this means of worshipping the gods, and if we are to understand sacrifice we have to look for the presuppositions that lie sometimes below the conscious surface of their minds. The most consistent misunderstanding in modern studies is that sacrifice can be defined in only one sense, or given only one kind of meaning or rationale. In fact, in the religions of early Christian days, there were many different types of sacrifice, offered for different purposes and with different motives. We must begin by exploring the different types and the different meanings that they had. Only then can we begin to attempt to interpret Christian thinking on sacrifice.

For convenience, we shall look at the traditional religion of the Graeco-Roman culture first, and then compare and contrast the ideas found in the Old Testament, which was in some ways more influential in forming Christian ideas on the subject. We shall find a considerable variety of rituals, whose meaning can be classified into three main types: gift-sacrifices, communion-sacrifices, and sin-offerings: but, within each broad class, we shall find different

21

ways of understanding their function, differences produced, at least partly, by differing theological ideas, differing views on the nature of their God or gods. The complexity of the subject will in itself show up the error of those who attribute only one meaning to sacrifice.

In the ancient world, sacrifice did not simply mean slaughter of animals. It covered all forms of offering to the gods, like the first fruits of the harvest, wine, honey, flour, and so on, though slain animals were usually regarded as richer and better offerings—reasonably enough, since meat was a luxury item in those days. Sometimes, the offerings were not of food, but of statuettes or jewelry. Whatever the offerings were, the most common type of sacrifice in Greek religion was the *votive offering*.[2] The characteristic of this type was that a city, community, or individual made a kind of bargain with the gods. When in need or distress, or motivated by some selfish desire, they would vow to a particular god or goddess some gift or sacrifice, to be provided in the future if the god solved their present problem or satisfied their immediate greed. For example, before the battle of Marathon, the Athenians vowed to Artemis that, if they won, they would sacrifice to her she-goats equal in number to the number of enemy dead. So many were slain that the vow was paid off at the rate of five hundred per year, and they were still paying it off sixty years or so later![3] This sort of sacrifice has been described as a 'business transaction'.[4] A man petitions the gods on the basis of how many sacrifices he has offered or will offer in return for the answer to his prayers. The gods are obligated to help men by their acceptance of these sacrifices. Sacrifices were bribes.

Behind this idea of sacrifice, there is clearly a very crude and primitive notion of the nature of the gods. Throughout the history of ancient Greece, common people regarded sacrifices as a means of *feeding* the gods. The ordinary worshipper thought that the gods were dependent on sacrifices for their food; they were displeased if they were forgotten, and kept in a good humour if a feast was provided. This idea of sacrifice was criticized by the more sensitive and intelligent at a very early date (as we shall see in the next chapter), but it was remarkably persistent. A highly educated Christian philosopher who wrote in the early third century told the Christians that if they offered sacrifices to the pagan gods, they were helping to feed the evil daemons, so giving sustenance to the enemy forces.[5] This argument was used to scare ordinary Christians from betraying their faith and giving way to the demand that they perform an act of sacrifice. Even where people rejected the idea that the gods were dependent on sacrifices, they still imagined that the gods enjoyed an occasional feast and still regarded sacrifice as a means of winning their favour. Sacrifice, then, was often understood as a *gift*, offered more or less as a bribe.

Considering what we have already discovered about Greek religious ideas, we shall not be very surprised to discover that they also understood sacrifice as a means of buying off the anger of a god. They offered *sacrifices of placation or propitiation*. Their concept of a god had not moved beyond seeing him as a bigger and better human being. So the gods sometimes got angry, often for no particularly moral reason, and their anger had to be appeased. It was not unnatural for Christ's sacrifice to be understood in this way among ordinary Gentile Christians, as we shall see.

Nevertheless, higher religious notions were also present in Greek religion. The great city festivals held in honour of the gods were occasions of worship, rejoicing, feasting, and thanksgiving. The animals slaughtered in sacrifice were shared. Worshippers had communion with the god in a feast, eating the meat and offering special portions to him on the altar. The god was present as a sort of head of the family; all feasted together, and the worshippers praised the greatness of the god and thanked him for his protection and support. These were *sacrifices of worship and thanksgiving*. So was the offering of the first fruits at harvest-time, for this expressed gratitude to the power which had made the crops grow and provided a successful harvest. Sacrifice was the only known means of expressing thanksgiving. It is natural to express gratitude by throwing a party or giving a present. And the people of the ancient world did the same in order to express gratitude to their gods.

There were *communion-sacrifices* of another type. The classic example of these is found in the religion of Dionysus, described so dramatically in Euripides' play *The Bacchae*. Here we see ecstatic and frenzied worshippers wandering over the mountains, tearing at the raw flesh of a bull. The bull was the incarnation of the god, and by eating its flesh, the worshipper received a little of the god's character and power. The play was written four hundred years before Christ, but many have pointed out the parallel with eating Christ's flesh in the eucharist.

There were other, more superstitious ideas. The worshippers *shared* in sacrifices offered to the gods; but there were other sacrifices in which the worshippers did not share. The 'holocaust' was burnt whole or buried whole in the ground. It was offered to evil spirits, to ghosts, to the spirits of the dead, and the object of the offering was to keep them away, to avert their influence which caused disease, old age, death, and other evils. These rites were performed at night, with 'shuddering' rather than joy.[6] These superstitious practices survived all through the early centuries of Christianity. Wearing charms to keep away evil influences derives from the same outlook. We shall discover later that some people thought of Christ's sacrifice in this way, as a sacrifice to scare away the devil. We shall call this type *aversion-sacrifices*, because their object was to avert.

So there was no single concept of sacrifice, no single understanding of what it accomplished. For the most part, however, in popular religion, the gods were thought of in very human terms and sacrifices were regarded as bribes or payments offered to keep a tyrant happy and propitious. It all seems rather crude and primitive, perhaps, but it remained so for the average uneducated peasant or workman. We have already remarked, however, that the whole system was criticized by the more sensitive and intelligent from very early on. To this discussion we shall turn in the next chapter.

But first let us look at the sacrifices of the Old Testament. Here we shall find rituals and types of sacrifice which clearly originated from similar primitive notions, but beliefs about them were transformed by the quite different theological context in which they continued to be practised. The God of Abraham, Isaac, and Jacob was less arbitrary than the play-boy gods of the Greeks.

The Old Testament has a rich and complex vocabulary describing an enormous variety of offerings and sacrifices. It is possible, however, to classify them into three types, along the same general lines as our analysis of Greek sacrifices. In doing this, we follow the precedent of a distinguished Jewish scholar named Philo, who was contemporary with Jesus of Nazareth.

The first category is *communion-sacrifices*. The rituals will be found in chapters 3 and 7 of Leviticus. Originally these sacrifices were performed at local altars whenever meat was eaten. Meat meant a feast, a special occasion, and God's bounty and gift of food, they felt, should not be enjoyed without including him in the festivities. Those who partook had to be in a state of ritual purity, that is, fit to feast in the presence of God. These sacrifices are close to the first type of communion-sacrifice described in Greek religion. The communion consists in fellowship, sharing a meal, not partaking of the divine life itself, as in the Dionysiac type. The relationship of guest and host established a special bond, and the communion-sacrifices of the Old Testament were realizations of the special covenant-bond which existed between God and his chosen people, the 'peace' between God and his worshippers.

This type of sacrifice in fact gradually lost importance in Israelite religion. When sacrificial worship had been centralized at the Jerusalem temple (one of the innovations of the book of Deuteronomy), provisions for the secular slaughter of animals outside Jerusalem had to be made (Deut. 12.15ff.), and no longer was every meat-meal a sacrificial feast.

In origin these communion-sacrifices were based on the assumption which lived on so long in pagan religion, that God ate his portion of the meat. But there are very few references to this idea in the Old Testament as it is now. More commonly sacrifice is said to provide a 'sweet savour' for God. This is a 'fossilized' expression which implies little more than God's pleasure in the devotion of his worshippers. It was inconceivable to the Jew that God who was author of all things could be dependent on men for anything, and in the final editions of the Law-books such crude ideas just do not appear.

The second category is 'holocaust', whole-burnt offerings (Lev. 1). These holocausts were *sacrifices of praise and thanksgiving*, of worship offered to God. The only similarity with the Greek 'holocaust' is the fact that the whole animal was offered. In other respects, there is no connection whatever. A closer parallel is the gift-sacrifice, though even in making this comparison we must beware, because in fact the motives were very different. The gift in Greek religion was intended as a bribe, whereas for the

Jew, to offer God the whole animal was an act of homage; it was the best possible sacrifice, the most perfect and complete. After the exile, the priests offered daily burnt-offerings on behalf of the nation. They were a continual act of praise to God. Some criticisms that we find in the prophets suggest that people occasionally thought of these as a means of buying God's favour,[7] but in most of the Old Testament this attitude is completely unknown. They simply believed that since man owes everything to God, it is right to pay tribute to him, and tribute meant giving up something vital from a man's flocks or herds, from his crops, or later from his money, in order to honour God.

It was the third type of sacrifice which dominated the Temple rituals in the time of Christ. The prophetic inter-pretation of the exile as God's judgement on his dis-obedient people heightened the sense of national sin and emphasized the need for constant expiation to prevent such a disaster occurring again. So after the exile in Babylon, *sin-offerings* (Lev. 4–7) came into prominence, and this development even affected the meaning of the 'holo-causts', to which expiatory significance was also transferred. The compilers of the Priestly Code, who produced the final edition of the Law-books, saw themselves as upholding exact and strict observances given by God to keep the covenant in being. Defilement annulled it. The prosperity of the nation depended on the removal of impurities, and this was the object of these offerings. In the case of deliberate or pre-meditated refusal to obey the Law, the offender was literally removed from the covenant-people by excom-munication; there was no means of atonement. But for the countless unintentional infringements of the Law, for the ritual pollution of the altar, the sacred vessels, the priests, the nation or the individual, sin-offerings could effect cleansing, and so cultic and moral purity be maintained. The God-given means of expiation was the sacrificial blood :

'The life of the flesh is in the blood, and I have given it for you upon the altar to make atonement for your souls; for it is the blood that makes atonement by reason of the life' (Lev. 17.11). God makes expiation for the land of his people (Deut. 32.43). The sin-offerings were not human attempts to buy off the anger of a righteous and vindictive God; they were not propitiatory, in the sense that they were an attempt to change God. Rather they were a means given by God himself for wiping away the sins which prevented his chosen people from fulfilling the obligations of the covenant-relationship and offering him fitting worship.

In addition to these three types of sacrifice offered continuously, there were a number of special Jewish feasts with their own sacrificial rites. For the most part these were more elaborate versions of the rites we have been discussing, but two 'primitive' survivals reflect a somewhat different view of sacrifice, a view very close to the *aversion-sacrifices* we found in pagan religion.

The Passover story is well-known (Exod. 12). God gave the command to Moses that each household should slaughter a lamb, smear its blood on the door-posts of the house, roast it and eat it with unleavened bread and bitter herbs. They were to be dressed ready for escape. The Angel of Death came and slew the first-born in Egypt, except where the sign of the blood protected the inmates. The story was celebrated year after year at the Passover festival. Whatever the historical events lying behind this story, it is clear that the blood of the lamb originated in a form of aversion-ritual. It was a magic potion to keep away the evil power. In Jewish tradition, this significance was lost. The celebration of Passover changed and developed, and stressed the saving act of God above everything else. But we shall find the primitive meaning revived in early Christian interpretation.

28

The Day of Atonement was late in development and was really a sort of annual 'super-sin-offering'. The rituals will be found in Leviticus 16 and 23. The special feature of the sin-offering was that the High Priest on this one and only occasion entered the Holy of Holies and sprinkled the atoning blood even on the mercy-seat over the ark of the covenant. In addition to this, however, the ancient scape-goat ritual was performed. Over a goat the High Priest confessed all the sins of Israel, and then it was banished into the desert, bearing them all away. This goat was 'for Azazel'; in the apocryphal book of Enoch, Azazel is des-cribed as the 'prince of the devils'.[8] The idea seems to have been originally an aversion-rite, sending off evil and sin to its source. This primitive meaning is much modified in Jewish literature; the rite was seen as a God-given means of removing the sins of his people, like the other sin-offerings. But again, the original meaning reappears in Christian interpretation.

In this chapter, we have traced a number of different types of sacrifice in the religious background in which Christianity grew up. They vary in sophistication, and their differences are to some extent due to different concepts of the divine nature, the god to which the offering is made. To interpret Christian ideas, we need to bear in mind the range of meanings given to sacrificial acts. The follow-ing summary draws together the various kinds of sacrifice we have discovered:

1. *Communion-sacrifices* are found in the Old Testament and in pagan religion. The worshippers share a feast with the god and offer him praise and thanksgiving. As Paul reminds us in I Corinthians 10.18, those who eat the sacrifices are sharers in the altar. In Greek religion, there were also communion-sacrifices of a different type, in which the worshippers actually partook of the god himself. Both

these types found some parallel in 'the table of the Lord', the Christian eucharist.

2. *Gift-sacrifices* were also offered in both traditions. The motives were different. For pagans, the gifts were often bribes; for the Jews they were offerings of praise and thanksgiving, a fitting tribute to their God. This type of sacrifice we shall find spiritualized in the Christian tradition, but also living on in certain material offerings, like the 'harvest-festival'.

3. *Sin-offerings* are found in Jewish and pagan religion, but here we find several different types:

(a) propitiatory offerings, which were offered to placate the anger of an offended deity (pagan, but traces of this idea in the Old Testament);

(b) aversion-sacrifices, offered to ward off the powers of evil (again pagan, but with traces surviving in Jewish rituals);

(c) expiatory offerings, sacrifices understood as a God-given means of wiping away sin and removing pollution (Jewish).[9]

Later we shall be using this analysis to interpret the sacrifices offered by the early Christians, and particularly their understanding of Christ's death on the cross as a sacrifice for sin. In conclusion, it is worth noting that the sacrifices described in our two modern novels reflect several of these types, and do not fall into the propitiatory pattern so often regarded as the right interpretation of sacrifice. The boys of the *Lord of the Flies* try to 'avert' the beast by offering sacrifice; Joseph's sacrifices in *To a God Unknown* express communion with his father, and a desire to 'expiate' the pollution of his land.

2

Non-Christian criticism, reinterpretation, and spiritualization of sacrifice

1

It is now possible to unearth to some extent the various layers of material in the Old Testament, from its most primitive strata to the final re-editing in terms of an increasing awareness of the true character of God and the demands of his worship. Ancient ritual phrases became invested with new meanings; we have already noted the 'sweet savour' example. Sacrificial rites are by nature conservative, but ideas are more flexible and change in the course of centuries. The main factor in transforming Hebrew ideas was the developing concept of God's universal sovereignty and righteousness. Such understanding of God's nature excluded crude conceptions of what happened when sacrifice was offered. So the form of worship remained much the same, but the attitude of the worshipper was transformed.

An early re-writing of the cult-laws in accordance with new concepts of God can be found in Deuteronomy. This was probably the result of the teachings of the prophets, who urged that it was unworthy of God to suppose that he was dependent on or needed sacrifices. According to Amos (4.4) and Jeremiah (7.21), it was not God who got pleasure from sacrificial feasts but the self-indulgent worshippers. What God demanded was obedience, and he did not need sacrifices.

In accordance with ideas of this kind, Deuteronomy reinterpreted the cultic ceremonies as the offering of fitting tribute to the God from whom all things had been received.

The various rites became memorials of God's saving acts in Israel's history, and the special covenant-relation which God had established with Israel. The rituals were filled with thoughts of what Israel owed to God rather than how to extort favours from him.[1] Sacrifice became an opportunity to acknowledge his goodness. So in the Old Testament, we can trace how the thoughts of the worshippers were turned away from any idea of seeking to change God's attitude or win his favour by offering sacrifices. Sacrifices were rather regarded as ordained by God to remind his people of his mercy and salvation.

Developments in the later Law-books can also be traced in some measure to the prophets. Their warnings that Israel was to suffer for her sins paved the way for the realization that their national God, Jahweh, was at least a superior God to those of other nations, and finally that he was the *only* God, Creator of all things. God, they came to believe, was the source of everything, good, evil, judgement, vengeance, *and* expiation (Deut. 32.39, 45). The idea that man by his own efforts could make adequate satisfaction for his sin was outlawed by stress on the sovereignty of God who alone could effect the expiation of sin and the purification of his people. At the same time, realization of God's holiness and power, in particular the realization that his wrath caused the exile, led to an increased concern with expiatory sacrifices so as to keep Israel free from catastrophe again. The wrath of God was not to be treated lightly. This is the sort of theology which moulded the rituals of the Priestly Code. God causes punishment for sin; God alone can get rid of sin; God gave sacrifice as a ritual means of dealing with sin.

As indicated, it is probable that these theological developments were due to the influence of the prophets. It is certain that the prophets had an influence on another matter, namely the development of Jewish thinking about the relationship between sacrifice and morality. Rich extortioners were observed making extravagant offerings in the belief that they would thus ensure God's blessing on their dubious enterprises. In opposition to this kind of thing, the prophets stressed that the sacrificial system was useless without moral virtues; they insisted on the superiority of justice, mercy, and love to all forms of material offering. They did not deny that God required service from his people, but they insisted that Israel was neglecting the one kind of service which God demanded, namely the end of oppression of the poor, acts of loving kindness, justice; only service of this kind would please God and ensure that he would listen to their prayers.[2] If the prophets had taken this to its logical conclusion and proposed a complete rejection of sacrifice, as some scholars have argued, they would have been far ahead of their time. In any case, that debate[3] is not immediately relevant, since such advice was certainly not followed, and the sacrificial system has theoretically never been rejected in Judaism. What is important is the fact that the teaching of the prophets inspired a counterbalancing strand of tradition in Jewish thought about sacrifice. On the one hand, the practice of sacrifice was sustained by the idea that it was ordained by God for the good of his people, but on the other hand, its subsidiary importance compared with a morally upright life was constantly stressed. The intention of the offerer was recognized as more important than the gift. It is particularly interesting that that part of Hebrew literature most closely associated with the daily cultic worship of the Temple, namely the Psalms,[4] contain this almost opposing strand of tradition. As hymns accompanying the processions and sacrificial rites, they gave expression to the meaning implicit in them; yet in doing so they insist that prayer and praise, and especially repentance and confession, are really more important.[5] The worshippers

33

are asked to admit that they cannot give God anything, for all things belong to him, and obedience to the Law is better than sacrifice.[6] The Psalms therefore always provided a corrective to the sacrificial worship that they accompanied. It is a broken spirit and contrite heart that God desires, though he also delights in sacrifices rightly offered (Ps. 51.16–19).

The Wisdom literature reflects the same moralizing tradition. Ecclesiasticus is a good example. The righteous man makes an offering simply by keeping the Law; alms-giving is a sacrifice of thanksgiving; atonement can be effected by abstention from wickedness (Ecclus. 35.1–10). So all the various types of literature which made up the Jewish scriptures were affected by this 'moralizing' tradition—Law, Prophets, Psalms, and Wisdom.

Thus, by the time of the Rabbis, it was integral to Jewish thinking, and it was just as well! For in A.D. 70 the Temple was sacked, and for all practical purposes this was the end of the sacrificial system. The Rabbis nevertheless were able to preserve the Jewish religion by drawing on their heritage. Rabbi Joshua felt moved to lament: 'Woe to us, for the place wherein the sins of Israel were expiated is destroyed.' But Rabbi Johanan ben Zakkai was able to reply: 'We still have a means of expiation of equal value— the practice of kindness, for it is said, "I will have kindness not offering".'[7] Prophetic teaching and the Psalms gave scriptural authority for asserting that good deeds, repentance, fasting, prayer and study of the Law were equivalent to sacrifice. It was axiomatic that God the Creator did not need sacrifice, and so emphasis was placed on the giver giving up something; fasting, in particular, became an adequate substitute.

It is perhaps scarcely surprising that away from Palestine this moralizing tradition had already become predominant. There were millions of Jews living scattered around the known world far from Palestine and the centralized Temple-cult. Just as there are Russian Jews, German Jews and American Jews today, so in the ancient world there were Alexandrian Jews and Roman Jews. Every major commercial city of the Empire had its Jewish ghetto, and in fact there were more Jews outside Palestine than in it. It is for this reason that we find Paul in Acts going to the Jewish synagogue or meeting-place in each city he visited, hoping to find there a base for his missionary activity. For these Jews, synagogue worship was all they really experienced, except perhaps for an occasional pilgrimage to Jerusalem. So prayer and virtue, rather than sacrifice, were for them a meaningful offering to God.[8] The synagogues had prepared the way for the survival of Judaism after the destruction of their central religious shrine.

This long-standing tradition that morality was more important than sacrifice was to become extremely important in early Christian thinking, as we shall see. As for the Rabbis, so for Christians, scriptural authority for the 'spiritualizing' of sacrifice was provided by the Old Testament. Besides this, the somewhat ambiguous language of the prophets made possible the assertion that God had never wanted or desired sacrifice, and thus provided justification for their rejection of material or literal performance of the Old Testament sacrificial law.

Another very important feature of Judaism, as far as background to Christianity is concerned, was a development from these 'spiritualizing' ideas. The offering of *oneself* became the ultimate sacrifice, and so the death of a martyr came to be regarded as sacrificial. A martyr's death, died in preference to denial of his religion, became equivalent to an expiatory sacrifice, and was regarded as a means of atoning for the sins of the nation.

The best-known example of this occurs in Isaiah 53. The spectators recognize that the servant died for their transgressions and was bruised for their iniquities. By the will of God, the servant made himself a sin-offering on their behalf. God laid on him the iniquity of all. The point becomes clearest, however, in the Maccabean literature. The Maccabees led a revolt against Greek tyrants who tried to Hellenize their subject peoples. In the books describing their exploits, we read stories of martyrs who refused to eat pork and so betray their Jewishness. The theory of these books is that Israel was suffering under the foreign yoke because of her sin (notice the influence of the prophets), and the deaths of her martyrs were able to expiate that sin. In 4 Maccabees (6.28ff.) Eleazar prays: 'Be merciful to thy people and let our punishment be a satisfaction on their behalf. Make my blood their purification, and take my soul to ransom their souls.'

In recent years, the discovery of the Dead Sea Scrolls has thrown further light on the contemporary situation into which Christianity came. Christianity began as a sect within Judaism. Here we seem to find another Jewish sect with remarkably similar views on sacrifice. The Dead Sea sect had broken with the official Temple, and found more spiritual ways of worship. We read such sentiments as these:

> They shall atone for guilty rebellion and for the sins of unfaithfulness that they may obtain loving kindness for the land, without the flesh of holocausts and the fat of sacrifice. And prayer rightly offered shall be an acceptable fragrance of righteousness and perfection of way a delectable freewill offering.[9]

All types of sacrifice, expiatory and thanksgiving in particular, are replaceable. Righteous living is capable of procuring God's favour and atonement, and prayer is 'an offering of the lips'. At first sight we appear to have a foreshadowing of the Christian rejection of sacrifice.

Phrases used are closely parallel and it is quite likely that there were direct contacts between this sect and the early Church.

Closer examination, however, reveals a fundamental difference. The reason for rejecting the practice of the Old Testament sacrificial law is far from the same. According to the Dead Sea Scrolls, the sect rejected sacrifice because they regarded the Temple as defiled by the Wicked Priest. They had excessively high standards of ritual purity, and thought of the Temple as polluted by the official Jewish hierarchy. Some passages anticipate the glorious future when God would enable the proper fulfilment of the Law according to their strict beliefs. So their attitude is not fundamentally different from orthodox Judaism. They cling to the belief that the Law is to be obeyed, and draw on the moralizing tradition to provide substitutes when something prevents proper fulfilment. By contrast, Christians soon developed a characteristically Christian 'theology' requiring the rejection of the sacrificial law of the Old Testament. We shall turn to this in the next chapter.

2

Meanwhile, sacrifice had also received plentiful criticism from the Greek philosophers, but they did not have the same influence as the prophets on the subsequent religious development of their compatriots. As late as the second century A.D., we find the satirist, Lucian, ridiculing the popular notions of sacrifice described earlier, in a somewhat lurid burlesque of current attitudes. He questions the piety of those who think so meanly of God as to suppose that he needs anything from the hands of men, takes pleasure in their flattery, or is wounded by their neglect. He pictures the gods in heaven looking down and waiting for sacrifices to be offered. If a sacrifice is being performed, all mouths are open to feed on the smoke. Like flies they settle on the altar, to drink up the trickling streams of blood.[10]

So the primitive notions persisted, but long before in literature the crude conceptions of God on which such notions depended had been modified. The gods were increasingly elevated to being the guardians of justice and morality, and sacrifice began to be connected with the moral sins of the worshipper rather than ancient taboos and impurities. Then acceptance of a more worthy concept of the gods and their morality led to criticism of popular attitudes to sacrifice. The famous philosopher, Socrates, insisted that sacrifice made no difference. Virtue alone was of value in the endeavour to keep the favour of the gods.[11] His influence was felt by all later philosophical ethics. Sacrifice with selfish, mercenary motives, such as to get riches or good health or a son and heir (and such things were the main content of popular petitions)—such sacrifice received its due criticism from a moral standpoint.

It also received criticism from a theological standpoint. It was unworthy of the dignity and sanctity of the gods. By this time it should be abundantly clear that the concept of God affected the attitude to and interpretation of sacrifice. If the gods were regarded as guardians of morality, then sacrifice could no longer be regarded as a bribe; such an understanding undermined their integrity. Well into the Christian era, we find taunts against the attempts to corrupt the gods by offering sacrifice.[12] Any concept of God, however crude, assumes that the gods are superior to men, and people began to see the absurdity of assuming that the gods were *dependent* on men for their food. Intelligent men realized that it was fantastic to think that the gods would starve if one did not sacrifice. The gods are above need; indeed they are above desire. They are independent of the offerings of men. The philosopher, Epicurus, developed this theological line to its most extreme conclusion, picturing the gods as immortal and happy and self-sufficient, totally unconcerned about men and whether they sacrificed or not. Such an idea, however, spells the death of religion.

Meanwhile attitudes were changing with the changes in politics. Under the rule of the emperors and kings, from Alexander the Great to the Romans, people somehow lost self-confidence and began to believe in fate, necessity or chance. Astrology became popular and increased the tendency towards a rigidly determinist outlook. A world ruled by fate and entirely predetermined is incapable of change. The object of sacrifice had been to effect a change in one's favour. So in this sort of cultural context, the practice of sacrifice was condemned by the philosophers as utterly illogical. Superstition was stronger than logic, however, and people even offered sacrifices to *Chance*, personified into a goddess.

More sophisticated philosophies also left no room for sacrifice. The Stoics believed in an impersonal Providence; virtue was the only thing that mattered, and virtue could be attained by a man's own efforts. Sacrifice was irrelevant. The Platonists insisted more and more on the Unchangeability of the one Supreme God of the Universe. So sacrifice was pointless: God would give each man his due, whether he prayed and sacrificed or not.[13] Nevertheless, for political reasons, in order to maintain social stability, all philosophers of this period were prepared to practice the traditional rites, and even endorse sacrifice to the divine emperor.[14]

In a very real sense, the philosophies of the period satisfied a *religious* need. For the old religion seemed crude and irrelevant. The educated intelligentsia thought more and more in terms of one unseen and unchangeable God behind the universe—absolute truth, absolute goodness, absolute beauty, already perfect, and therefore not subject to change or development. Sacrifice was therefore irrelevant, and so the religious man sought spiritual satisfaction in the 'philosopher's prayer'—intercourse between the divine being and the soul based on kinship and likeness.[15] It meant withdrawal from the changes and chances, the passions and desires of this world for contemplation of the Ultimate. So real religion became an internal, spiritual thing. Sacrifice ceased to have any *real* religious meaning. The philosopher sought a life of virtue by imitating the gods, while the gods were conceived in a more elevated and uplifting way.

All these tendencies culminated in Neoplatonism, a religious philosophy which summed up the highest aspirations of the Hellenistic world, and its search for something more religiously satisfying than the traditional cults. This philosophical school arose in the third and fourth centuries A.D. and became a direct rival to Christianity. The two 'philosophies' had much in common. Both believed in one Supreme God, the ultimate ground of the universe. The characteristics of this God followed the traditional conclusions of philosophy. He was primary in the sense that nothing preceded or caused him. He was immaterial and eternal. He was perfect and therefore changeless. He was beyond passion, emotion and need. He was entirely self-sufficient. The Christians added other characteristics drawn from scripture—like Creator of the world, loving, saving, etc. But philosophically, they all argued from the same presuppositions.

As we have seen, philosophy had long cast doubt on sacrifice, but in the conditions of the late Roman Empire Neoplatonism became the defender of an artificially unified paganism against the encroaching power and influence of the Christian Church. The Neoplatonic writings provide us with the most comprehensive discussion of sacrifice in ancient literature. Here we find the first real attempt to rationalize traditional religion and uphold it against the long-standing criticisms of it. The main points of their discussion ultimately came from the same sources, or were formulated under the same influences, as the Christian statements for and against sacrifice. Many interesting parallels can be found in Neoplatonist and Christian literature.

There are three aspects of the Neoplatonist discussion to which I wish to draw attention, bearing in mind its relevance to interpretation of Christian ideas:

1. The Neoplatonists insisted that whatever gifts were offered to God had to be worthy of him. In the early days of Neoplatonism, this principle led Porphyry to reject animal sacrifices; killing animals, he argued, is morally wrong, and it is impossible to think of the gods as demanding an immoral act as worship.[16] It also led him to distinguish between different grades of deity to whom different kinds of sacrifice are proper. To the Supreme God, we should not sacrifice, for even a word is too material a means. He can only be worshipped by pure silence, holy sacrifice being offered to him simply by close contact with him and being transformed into his likeness. There are, however, lower heavenly beings. To the highest of these gods may be offered hymns and words, the 'first-fruits' of beautiful thoughts. To beings lower down the scale, material offerings (other than animal sacrifice) should be offered according to ancestral custom.

Exactly the same principle, that gifts must be worthy of the deity to which they were offered, motivated Christian writers who claimed that only spiritual sacrifices could be worthy of the one true God. One early apologist insisted that worship that is worthy of God is not destruction of his gifts by fire, but thankful use of them for one's own good and for the needy, as well as prayer, praise, and thanksgiving.[17] In words that were echoed by Porphyry, a Christian philosopher, Clement of Alexandria, said that

41

the offering of oneself purified from sin and selfish emotions, honouring God by prayer, these are the only sacrifices that are worthy of God who needs nothing.[18]

2. The Neoplatonists recognized the existence of different types of sacrifice in traditional religion, along the lines of the analysis offered in the first chapter. They went on to reject or justify each type according to its consistency with their concept of God. Porphyry rejected propitiatory offerings, offerings intended to appease a god's anger, or change his mind, or win his favour.[19] These, he felt, were not consistent with the goodness and changelessness of the gods. On the other hand, sacrifices of worship and thanksgiving should be offered in honour of the gods. A later Neoplatonist, however, named Iamblichus, deliberately attacked Porphyry's position and sought justification and a rationale for *all* the traditional types of sacrifice—even the superstitious rites of aversion.[20]

These distinctions are important for understanding the Christian use of, or rejection of, the various types. Propitiation-sacrifices were consciously rejected by Christian philosophers, as they were by Porphyry, because they were inconsistent with their concept of God. But spiritual sacrifices of worship and thanksgiving constituted their religious and liturgical life.

3. It was important for the Neoplatonists to make traditional paganism relevant against the powerful claims of Christianity. Christian apologists did not hesitate to use the old maxims of philosophical criticism against the traditional cult-practices. So the Neoplatonists sought a rationale—a justification, a reasoned account of sacrifice which fitted with their higher and more philosophical concept of God. There could be no sense in which the gods were dependent on men for their sustenance or gratification; the gods could not be susceptible to sacrificial bribery and corruption. They

and their Christian contemporaries accepted this, and they combated crude, popular notions of sacrifice. God transcends the material world and has no need of material gifts. He does not lack or desire anything. But still, according to Iamblichus, it is right to offer the traditional sacrifices. The whole universe works together in sympathy and the rites are effective because of the common life and sympathetic union of all grades of being. The life of the sacrificed animal is a link between gods and men. As the fire assimilates the sacrifice to itself, so are we assimilated to the gods. 'Propitiation' does not change the gods, it converts men to participation in the divine life. Sacrifice is thus turned into an acted parable of the union and sympathy of the universe. Sacrificial rites are symbols of man's escape from the material world to assimilation with the gods.

Later on we shall see how similar were the ideas of early Christian philosophers. Christians rejected literal sacrifice, but they offered spiritual sacrifices and they saw Christ's death as the supreme sacrifice. So the problem with which they had to cope was: what was the point of sacrificing to a changeless and perfect God. They too suggested that 'propitiation' changed man, not God; they linked the sacrificial death of Christ with escape from evil and the restoration of unity with the divine.

Christian converts were drawn from all levels of society. Some came with the pretty crude ideas of traditional paganism about the gods and offerings to keep the gods happy, others with the accumulated wisdom of philosophy, steeped in the same traditions as the Neoplatonists. But all had to accommodate their minds to a very different outlook, namely the Jewish tradition enshrined in the Old Testament which the Church inherited as its scriptures. They had to pull together the threads which have run through this chapter.

But they were not the first to try to do this, nor the only ones. To a certain extent they were able to follow

43

where others had led. For Jews and Greeks did not live in separate sealed compartments in the Roman Empire. Already cultural contacts had been widespread.

We have already seen that Jews lived all over the Graeco-Roman world. This Diaspora (Dispersion) of the Jews meant that already cultured Greek-speaking Jews read the Old Testament in a Greek translation and interpreted it in terms of the cultural setting in which they lived. Vice versa, some pagans were attracted by the monotheism and high moral code of the Jews, and their religion or philosophy was influenced by this. Two examples illustrate this 'syncretism' or conflation of culture, and provide very important parallels to the developments in Christianity.

1. About the time of Christ, there lived a Jewish philosopher, Philo, in the Greek city of Alexandria at the mouth of the Nile. He thought and spoke in Greek; he had received a typical education in the literature and philosophy of the Greek classics and their contemporary interpretation. So he thought in the categories of the Hellenistic culture. But he was also a practising Jew. He combined the best in both traditions as far as sacrifice is concerned. He inherited and emphasized the Jewish insistence that morality is more important; he followed the ideal of the 'philosopher's prayer'. He revered Temple-worship as ordained by God in his Law, but interpreted the sacrifices as really being symbols of the offering of spiritual and moral virtues. God does not rejoice in sacrifices, he affirmed, for all things are in his possession, and because he possesses all things, he is in need of none. Justice is more important than sacrifice; prayer is a higher form of worship. 'God rejoices in altars without fires, around which virtues dance.' It is impossible to give God anything apart from praise.[21] Philo foreshadows the viewpoint of the Christian Church, especially in his 'spiritualizing' or symbolical interpretation of the Law-

books of the Old Testament, finding there his own philosophical religion. In one particular he differed. As a Jew, he did not reject the practice of sacrifice, even though his interpretation devalued its literal performance.

2. Another witness to the cross-fertilization of religious culture is found in the Hermetic Corpus. This group of writings probably dates from the early third century, but parts are almost certainly older, and the religious ideas expressed older still. They are supposed to be accounts of special revelations of the god Hermes. In other words, we are dealing here with pagan literature. Hermes was the traditional messenger of the gods in Greek mythology. In these tracts, however, Hermes appears with revelations about creation with details clearly based on the Genesis account. He calls the reader to a life combining the ideals of Greek philosophy and Jewish ethics. In these documents we find a radical spiritualization of sacrifice. God needs nothing; he is everything and all things are in him. We should adore him by giving thanks. Even burning incense, the purest form of material sacrifice, is regarded as an abomination to God who is above all matter. Material sacrifice is abolished and replaced by 'rational sacrifices' (compare Paul in Romans 12.1, where almost exactly the same words appear). These spiritual sacrifices are interpreted as consisting in the ecstasy of worship, or moral qualities.[22] These ideas are extremely close to Christian ideas and witness to the quality of pagan religious thought prior to the anti-Christian reaction in the succeeding generations, reflected in the writings of Iamblichus.

So by this time, Greek philosophy was influencing the ideas of some Jews, and Judaism was influencing the religious philosophy current in sophisticated circles. In the early Christian centuries, then, Greek philosophy and contemporary Judaism alike aspired to a purely spiritual religion. But alongside this there was a reluctance to over-turn the long-established practices of the traditional cults. Jews of course opposed idolatry and the rites of paganism, but they never abandoned sacrifice, at least in theory, because it was prescribed in the Law of God. Philosophers compromised on political or social grounds. Christians alone stood out against all sacrificial rites, and at least aspired to practise a purely spiritual religion. Christians became a 'third race', bridging the cultures of Jew and Greek, assimilating ideas from each, rejecting the practices of both. The next chapter will elucidate Christian ideas in the light of the background study so far pursued.

3
Sacrifice in the early Church

Up to now we have been attempting to outline the contemporary context in which Christian thought about sacrifice developed. Now we turn to study more closely the actual position of the early Church, to examine the process by which both Jewish and pagan sacrifices were rejected, though on quite different grounds, and to discover how, in the development of a cult proudly proclaimed as spiritual and contrasted with the inferior material worship of contemporary religions, Christianity actually assimilated many of the ideas we have already outlined.

1

THE REJECTION OF SACRIFICE

A. *The Church and Jewish sacrifices*
The Church was in origin a sect of Judaism, founded by Jesus of Nazareth, who appeared as a new prophet for the house of Israel, calling for repentance and reform in the conviction that the kingdom of God was dawning. Judaism was therefore the starting-point of Christian ideas. For this reason we examine first the reasons why Christians rejected the Jewish Temple-cult.

We may begin by inquiring what Jesus thought about sacrifice. According to the gospel traditions, Jesus never made any formal repudiation of sacrifice, but he did adopt the prophetic point of view that morality was of far greater importance. In the context of Pharisaic Judaism, this took the form of criticism of excessive preoccupation with minute observances of the Law, a preoccupation which only emphasized that the Pharisees had failed to understand the

47

prophetic saying, 'I desire mercy, and not sacrifice' (Matt. 9.13; 12.3). He accused them of being so concerned with outward cleanliness that they neglected inward purity (Mark 7.1–23; Matt. 23.25–8). In the eyes of Jesus, the scribe who said that love of God and of one's neighbour was more important than burnt-offerings and sacrifices was not far from the kingdom of God (Mark 12.33–4). He applied rigidly the principle that the right attitude is necessary when sacrificing—a mere quarrel with one's brother makes a sacrifice invalid (Matt. 5.23–4). To escape the responsibility of helping aged parents by declaring all financial support owed them 'Corban'—that is, dedicated to God as a sacrificial gift—was a serious misuse of the sacrificial law (Mark 7.9–13).

In other words Jesus was concerned with abuses of the Law. This is confirmed by the cleansing of the Temple. This incident was not a repudiation of Temple-worship and the sacrificial system, though later it received this interpretation. Rather it was a protest against turning the place of prayer into a profitable market-place and banking-exchange. One saying recorded in the tradition represents Jesus as believing, like his contemporaries, that the Temple was sacred as the special dwelling-place of God (Matt. 23.21), but unlike other people, he drew the consequences that it was a scandal that the house of prayer had been turned into a den of robbers.

Although Jesus is portrayed in the Gospels as critical of Pharisaism and as being himself independent of the details of the Jewish Law, he, like the prophets of old, frequented the normal places of worship, the synagogues and the Temple. The early Jerusalem Church, unlike the community depicted in the Dead Sea Scrolls, did not break with the Temple-worship. The features of the Church recorded in Acts include not only the breaking of bread, prayers, and communal living, but also daily attendance at the Temple. It was there that Peter and John cured the lame beggar and roused the ire of the authorities. The Church behaved in the first instance like a community of orthodox Jews, which suggests that Jesus did not openly reject the traditional religious rites of Judaism.

But very early on a conflicting point of view appeared. There can be little doubt that Jesus, like the prophets earlier, predicted disaster if the nation did not repent, and one of the things he threatened was the destruction of the Temple (Mark 14.58; John 2.19). A group of Hellenized Jews, converted to the gospel, took this to mean that as followers of Jesus they should reject the Temple-worship. Stephen seems to have preached that Temple-worship was a form of idolatry, applying the arguments against sacrifice, drawn from Jewish polemic and Greek philosophy, against not merely pagan cults but the Jewish cult as well (Acts 6 and 7). But this line of thought was not predominant in the early stages. Peter, the other apostles, and also James, the brother of Jesus, who quickly became head of the Jerusalem Church, maintained an orthodox Jewish position. Even Paul behaved as a Jew and underwent purificatory rites in the Temple, making requisite sacrifices and bearing the expense for four other Jews who were under a vow (Acts 21.23–6).

As Christianity spread outside Jerusalem, the importance of sacrifice and the Temple-worship naturally decreased. It was soon decided that Gentiles could become members of the Church without becoming Jews first, without being circumcised and undertaking to keep the whole of the Jewish Law. The Church modelled its worship on the Jewish synagogue rather than the Temple-cult; so there was no sacrifice. In this world-wide context, however, Paul had already begun to use sacrificial language to describe the worship and service of Christians, in much the same way as the Jews of the Dispersion already did. Besides this, he

49

had also used sacrifice as a means of understanding the death of Christ. In the Epistle to the Hebrews, this approach was taken further, so much so that it amounted to a rejection of Jewish sacrifices *on principle*, and the principle was an entirely new one. It was not just acceptance of the old criticisms of the practice. It was an assertion that *Christ's sacrifice had replaced them*. Sacrifice should no longer be offered by Christians, not because Christ's message was in conflict with the Old Testament revelation of the past, but because he had so fulfilled it as to make it meaningless. This message was delivered, as far as we can tell, to Jewish Christians who were tempted to return to their old faith, and the author clearly regards their desire to perform the old sin-offerings and rituals of the Day of Atonement as a denial of salvation in Christ, a rejection of the gospel, indeed as apostasy. By this time, the Church was no longer a sect of orthodox Judaism. Jewish religious practices were rejected *on principle*. The sacrificial system was not condemned but shown to be wanting; ultimately only the death of Christ fulfilled the purpose of the Law. Jewish sacrifices were to be rejected, not simply on negative, critical grounds, like the early group around Stephen, but because of a new interpretation of sacrifice in the light of Christ's death on the cross.

This epistle was produced in crisis, perhaps the persecution by Nero in Rome, or more probably the Jewish War of A.D. 66-70. It seems to have been this event which finally split the Church and Judaism; for Christian Jews refused to support the nationalist revolt. The rejection of Judaism was sealed by the re-interpretation of the whole of the Old Testament in terms of Christ. The Church never went back after this. The fall of the Temple in A.D. 70 was seen as God's judgement on the Jews for rejecting Christ, and all the subsequent early Christian literature follows the argument that the sacrificial law, the ritual observances, the Temple-worship, etc. had been all annulled by their fulfilment in the New Covenant, the new Israel, the Church. In working out the details of this fulfilment, the Church developed a completely spiritualized cult. Many of the ideas were drawn from the spiritualizing movements outlined before, but the basic reason for the rejection of sacrifice was the view that the death of Christ was the one perfect sacrifice rendering all others unnecessary. This was the new and distinctive element in Christian understanding, and the feature which was absolutely central to the whole thing.

It was in the light of this new thinking that the Cleansing of the Temple was reinterpreted as a rejection of the Jewish cult, and the rebuilding of the Temple understood as the resurrection of the Body of Christ (John 2.21), or the building of a spiritual temple within Christians.[1] There were christological grounds for the rejection of Jewish sacrifices.

B. *The Church and pagan sacrifices*

The Church also rejected pagan sacrifices, but on quite different grounds. As early as Paul's missionary journeys, the new Christian movement came into contact with paganism. At this stage, the Church was still really Jewish. Its converts were Gentiles who were already on the fringes of the synagogues, interested in a monotheistic religion with more ethical content than the unsatisfying religions of their own culture. In this context, it was inevitable that Christians adopted Jewish polemic against idolatry and reacted strongly against the local cults and sacrifices to idols. Very quickly the philosophical criticisms of sacrifice were combined with Jewish arguments. In Paul's sermon at Athens (as reported in Acts 17.22ff.), we find Jewish scorn of the worship of idols made of wood, metal or stone by human craftsmen (an attitude which goes back to Deutero-

Isaiah) and, alongside, typical philosophical arguments, such as the point that God cannot dwell in temples made with hands. The 'philosophers' Paul addressed found all this quite acceptable; it was only the preaching of the resurrection which alienated them. Christianity was heir to the climate of thought produced by contacts between Judaism and Greek philosophy, as outlined in the last chapter. Acts tells us that at Ephesus the population rioted because the message of the travelling preachers meant the end of their prosperous trade associated with the cult of Diana. Christians were as uncompromising as Jews in their insistence that worship should only be offered to the one true God. Hence Paul's problem in 1 Corinthians (8–10), where his Gentile converts could not quite see why the Christian attitude to the eating of idol-meat was so strict. 'We know the idols are not really gods, that the gods do not really exist', they seem to have argued; 'so why should we not just eat the meat, like most of the philosophers do, irrespective of whether the meat has been offered in sacrifice or not?' But the Jew in Paul could not accept that argument, however logical. The idols may be nothing, but we must beware of giving the impression that we are false to the one, true God.

Christians demonstrated their protest against pagan sacrifices in two ways: (i) their refusal to eat meat sacrificed in pagan temples and then sold in the market-place; and (ii) by refusing to offer even a token amount of incense as a show of political loyalty. Their attitude was absolutely uncompromising, and it was taken over from their predecessors, the Jews. The difference was, however, that those who were Jews by race as well as by religion were tolerated by Rome and allowed to be conscientious objectors; but the majority of Christians were very soon not Jews, either by race or religion. They were renegade pagans. So their refusal to sacrifice was taken as obstinacy and dangerous to the state. To the world at large, the Christian position was inexplicable. Because they would neither accept the traditional cults of the cities, nor were Jews, nor apparently offered sacrifice as part of their own worship, they were regarded as atheists, and all the emotions of superstitious crowds were easily aroused against them. In times of persecution, the Christians could gain no impartial hearing, because their opponents and their judges were inspired not only by prejudice, but also by unreasoning fear of the gods. On their side, Christian opposition to sacrifice was also intensified by fear and emotion. As already mentioned, Christian teachers warned that idolatry was not merely the most grievous sin, but highly dangerous, since the evil daemons were fed by the sacrifices; to sacrifice to them was to nourish them and help increase their strength for evil work in the world. Thus, popular notions were used to reinforce the converts in their stand against their past beliefs and practices.

So Christians were in the position of having no sacrificial practices recognized as such in the Roman world. In place of this a purely spiritual cult satisfied the religious needs of the converts, and in developing this the Church drew on the traditions of Judaism and Greek philosophy outlined in earlier chapters.

2

THE DEVELOPMENT OF A SPIRITUAL CULT

The spiritual cult was the offering of prayers, the spiritual altar was the mind of faithful Christians, and spiritual images of God were the virtues implanted in men by Christ. The body of Christ was a spiritual Temple. The Christian people continually celebrated feasts by constant prayer and fasts by abstention from wickedness. Above all, Christ himself was the perfect sacrifice and the High Priest through whom Christian prayers were offered. The Christians claimed that they *did* have a cult, but it was entirely immaterial.[2]

To look at these spiritualizing ideas more closely and to come to grips with the real meaning of sacrifice in the early Church, we need to approach the matter from several different angles. We need to distinguish those elements drawn from the Jewish background, those drawn from pagan philosophy, and those elements which are distinctive. We also have to see whether Christian sacrifices can be analysed into types in the same way as the literal sacrifices we were exploring earlier.

A. Jewish background

The first thing we can be sure of is that the Church adopted the 'prophetic moralizing' tradition in a very radical form. We have already seen that this played a considerable part in the teaching of Jesus, though it was not at that stage accompanied by a rejection of sacrifice. It is not surprising to find that, as Jews faced the loss of the Temple by drawing on this tradition, so Christians turned to it to find scriptural backing for their spiritual cult. Paul adopted this line of thought, regarding acts of charity as a suitable alternative to animal sacrifice. The financial help sent to him by the Philippians he describes as a 'fragrant offering' (using in fact the Old Testament phrase, a 'sweet savour'), a sacrifice acceptable and well-pleasing to God (Phil. 4.18). By complete obedience and faith, Christians were to present themselves, their bodies, as a living sacrifice, holy acceptable to God, which is your 'rational worship' (Rom. 12.1). Christians were to be holy and faultless in a moral sense, just as the sacrificial victims had been physically pure, according to the Law (e.g. Phil. 2.15–17). The Epistle to the Hebrews (13.15) speaks of a sacrifice of praise, the fruit of lips which confess his name, language which is very

54

reminiscent of the Dead Sea Scrolls. In the following verse (13.16), to do good and to share are described as sacrifices well-pleasing to God. The author adopts the Jewish view that just and charitable acts are as good as sacrifice. In a Christian work of the second century, fasting is described as a sacrifice; so is charity; and on a fast-day, Christians are advised to eat only bread and water, then reckon up what they would have spent on food and give it to widows, orphans or anyone else in need.[3] These ideas are clearly very close to those we have already found in Jewish literature where fasting and almsgiving were regarded as equivalent to sacrifice.

The Church adopted the Jewish scriptures, which became the Old Testament when Christian books were collected into a New Testament. In the early days, the Jewish scriptures were the scriptures of the Church. This is very important because the early Christians believed that they could find scriptural authority for their position with regard to sacrifice, especially in the Psalms and the prophets. The weight of scriptural authority helped to justify their 'spiritualizing' or 'moralizing' of sacrifice. Early Christian writers collected together the anti-sacrificial passages in the prophets[4] in order to show that God did not need or want the sacrifices of the Jews, but rather demanded obedience, learning to do good, desisting from evil, seeking justice, correcting oppression, and supporting the widow and orphan. A passage from the Book of Malachi (Mal. 1.11) proved to their satisfaction that Jewish sacrifices had been rejected and only Gentiles now made acceptable offerings —that is, the now predominantly Gentile Christian Church. These sacrifices were alone perfect and acceptable; they were sacrifices of prayer and thanksgiving, and the offering of the *eucharist*.[5] The Psalms were another good quarrying ground, especially Psalms 69, 50 and 51. Verse 17 was seen as the climax of Psalm 51: 'The sacrifice acceptable to God is a broken spirit, a broken and a contrite heart, God will not despise'; the following verses about offering sacrifice were ignored.[6] Phrases from the Psalms were linked into liturgical responses. One very early example runs as follows:

Sacrifice to the Lord is a broken heart,
Sweet savour to the Lord is a heart glorifying its Maker.[7]

This second phrase is not a direct quotation from the Old Testament, but it is built out of Old Testament idioms to produce a parallel clause to the first, to give liturgical expression to the offering of the spiritual sacrifice of repentance in worship.

The Church was also indebted to its Jewish past for another way of reinterpreting sacrifice. Christian martyrs, like the Jewish martyrs of the Maccabean literature, died sacrificial deaths; Christians were able, under persecution, to 'fill up what was lacking in the suffering of Christ' (Col. 1.24). It is highly probable that the tradition that a martyr's death could expiate sin was in fact the earliest positive means of understanding the death of Christ, as we shall see later. It was certainly the way in which Christians came to terms with their own sufferings for the gospel. The close connection between the Church and its Jewish past can easily be seen by means of a comparison between the early Christian martyr literature and the Maccabean books, which were clearly used as models for the early acts of the martyrs.[8] Christian preachers regarded the Maccabees as remarkable prototypes of Christian martyrdom.[9] They never ceased to be amazed that they died *before* being given the example of Christ, which was the chief inspiration to Christians. We have a very good example of Christian attitudes to martyrdom in the letters of Ignatius. He was an early bishop of Antioch, and around A.D. 110 he travelled to Rome to face martyrdom. On his journey he wrote seven letters to churches which he was passing. He speaks of his approaching death as a 'sacrifice of God', as a 'ransom' for the Church, using language from the Maccabean literature. He also speaks of wanting to 'follow the example of the passion of my God'.[10] This is the *new* element in the Christian attitude. The martyr saw himself as participating in the atoning sacrificial work of Christ.

B. The debt to Greek philosophy

There are few indications of the Church's debt to Greek philosophy in the New Testament. At this stage, the Church was tied to its Jewish background. However, as we have seen, there are hints in Stephen's speech in Acts 7, and Paul's speech in Acts 17. In both cases, the speakers appeal to the tradition that God does not dwell in temples made with hands, nor does he need or desire sacrifice. By this time such sentiments were commonplace where the Jewish and Greek cultures met.

The debt to Greek philosophy rapidly became very important, and much more obvious than the New Testament hints we have noticed. In the first place, Christian philosophers of the third century christianized the idea of the 'philosopher's prayer', understood as a life of imitation and contemplation of God, and separation from the material and earthly. Christian ideals became assimilated to the philosophical ideal. God is changeless, above the storms of passion and emotion, indeed perfect. The soul yearns to escape from the changes and chances of life, to be above passions and emotions, to imitate God. As for the philosophers, so for the Christians, this imitation of God became the perfect sacrifice. One Christian[11] wrote that God should be worshipped not with blood and fleshly sacrifices, but in spirit. He ridiculed the idea that a God who is known spiritually should be worshipped in a material way. The language of the Christian writers of the third century and later is very similar to that which we found in the Neo-platonists. The idea was to cut oneself off from sin, from emotion—in fact from involvement with earthly concerns, to achieve perfect contemplation of the divine as the only sacrifice worthy of God. This ideal became even more prominent when the Christian Church became respectable and persecution ceased. Monasticism, withdrawal from the world and its passions and desires, then replaced martyrdom as a means of finding personal sanctification, as a means of offering oneself as a pure sacrifice to God.

In the second place, apologists for Christianity made use of philosophical criticisms of sacrifice, and contrasted the crude pagan rites with their own better way of worship. It became a commonplace in Christian argumentation that God could not be dependent on men for his food, or his pleasure. He far transcends the material world and has no need of material gifts. He lacks nothing, nor desires anything, being beyond passions and pleasures. It is man who needs to worship God, not God who receives anything by it.[12] The apologists also adopted the argument that God could not be bribed or bought off by sacrificial gifts. He is just, he is perfect, he is changeless. No sacrifice can alter his attitude to men. The Christian philosopher, Clement of Alexandria, sums up in words very reminiscent of the pagan philosophers: 'The Divine nature is not wanting in anything, nor is it fond of pleasure or gain or money, being itself full and affording all things to every creature which is in need. So the Divine nature cannot be propitiated by sacrifices or offerings, nor is it allured by them.'[13]

Now the consequence of this argumentation was that the interpretation of sacrifice as a means of 'propitiating' God became unacceptable. Like the philosophers, the more sophisticated Church members rationalized the crude ideas naturally brought into the Church by pagan converts, the idea that God was angry; that sacrifices were meant to appease him. The arguments of Christian philosophers indicate that, much to their distaste, even the spiritual sacrifices of the Church were frequently understood in this way. Clement's successor, Origen, wrote a treatise *On Prayer*, which is almost entirely in the philosophical tradition, justifying prayer against all the arguments that it is useless because God is changeless.

Thirdly, we can see the influence of the philosophical tradition in the fact that the Christians, like the Neoplatonists, were anxious that their offerings should be worthy of God as they now conceived him. One early apologist, as we have already seen, insisted that worship that is worthy of God is not destruction of his gifts by fire, but thankful use of them for the good of oneself and of the needy, as well as prayer and praise and thanksgiving. The only worthy offering is *oneself* purified from sin and selfish emotions, according to Clement.[14] These are the only sacrifices worthy of God, who needs nothing. Augustine, the great Western theologian of the late fourth century, quoted a passage summarizing the right attitude to sacrifice and worship,[15] and the words he quotes are not from a Christian author, but a Neoplatonist, Porphyry: 'For God, indeed, being the Father of all, is in need of nothing; but for us it is good to adore him by means of justice, charity and other virtues, and thus to make life itself a prayer to him, by inquiring into and imitating his nature. For inquiring purifies us, and imitation deifies us, by moving us close to him.'

So we find that Christianity was indebted to its Jewish past and its philosophical environment. Where, we may ask, is its originality, the 'new thing'? Is it all adopted from elsewhere?

Not by any means. We can trace several distinctive points.

1. We have already referred to the fact that Christians

found themselves in a sort of 'limbo' between two cultures, and met the prejudice of both sides. They refused to compromise with the social and political order, as the philosophers did. Yet they did not have the legal protection of being Jews. Therefore they were persecuted. Their position was the result of an unique combination of 'spiritualizing' ideas with the Jewish tradition of uncompromising monotheism.

2. If we compare the writings of the philosophers, even Jewish philosophers like Philo, with the Christian philosophers, we find a change in emphasis which is quite marked. There are many ideas in common, like the four cardinal virtues: temperance, courage, justice, wisdom. All alike seek purity of soul, virtue, passionlessness. They all in common regarded hymns, praises, and prayers as spiritual means of worship. But Christian lists add the virtues of charity, care for others, almsgiving, love, martyrdom, and these are in fact given greater emphasis. The reason for this is that the central focus of the Christian spiritual cult was *Jesus Christ and his sacrifice*. An example of this transfer of emphasis reads as follows:

> Each of us is our own whole-burnt offering [in the Old Testament sense of total sacrifice of praise and thanksgiving], if we renounce everything and take up our cross and follow Christ, if we give our body to be burned, having charity, and follow the glory of martyrdom ...[16]

So there were distinctive elements, and the most distinctive of all was the sacrifice of Christ, which we shall be examining in more detail in the next chapter. Apart from this, what were the main features of the Christian spiritual cult? Many characteristics we have already observed in our discussions in this chapter, but it is worth mapping them out for greater clarity, and to get the overall

conspectus. In order to do this, and to appreciate, at the
same time, the variety of sacrificial ideas and intentions in
the early Church, it is worth referring back to the type-
analysis we traced earlier. We have seen that there was no
single meaning of sacrifice in the ancient world—rather
there were different types with different meanings. Many
Christian writers were fully aware of the different types,
like their Neoplatonist contemporaries. So we are justified
in using our type-analysis in order to set out a summary
of the Christian spiritual cult.

SACRIFICES OF PRAISE, WORSHIP AND THANKSGIVING
(Jewish type of gift-sacrifice)

A. First-fruit offerings

Christians did in fact bring first-fruit offerings in kind,
even though they repudiated animal sacrifice. The first-fruit
offerings were a sort of 'harvest-festival', though celebrated
much more frequently. We have evidence[17] that whenever
bread was baked or a jar of olive-oil opened, the 'first-fruits'
were set aside and offered to the prophets or priests of the
Church, or else given away in charity. These gifts were
brought to the altar and dedicated, to render thanks to
God and praise to the Creator. These 'sacrifices' were therefore not entirely spiritualized, though the material offerings
were sublimated by their object, which was charity or
the support of ministers of the Church, rather than crude
destruction by fire on the altar. So, in a sense, they were
spiritualized. The eucharistic offering was seen as closely
parallel to these other offerings in kind, and therefore, in
one sense, was a gift-sacrifice of worship and thanksgiving.
It was called a first-fruit offering.[18]

B. The offering of worship

The most common sacrifices of thanksgiving and praise

offered by the Church were the hymns, prayers, psalms, and praises of Christian worship. It was these that were so frequently contrasted with the worship of other religions, as being truly spiritual, rather than material.

C. The offering of self

For the individual Christian, the offering of *oneself* was the supreme sacrifice. Martyrdom was at first the ultimate self-offering, but with the end of persecution it was replaced by monasticism, withdrawal from the world and total self-denial. But the ordinary Christian too could make a sacrifice by living a life of Christian virtue. These were sacrifices of total praise, worship, and thanksgiving, offered in imitation of Christ's total self-offering.

SACRIFICES OF COMMUNION

A. The fellowship meal

There is evidence[19] that the Church celebrated fellowship meals, in which the food eaten was consecrated to God and shared with the bishop of the local community. Again this was a material offering in a sense, though no animal-sacrifice or meat-eating was associated with it. It was a 'semi-spiritualized' communion-sacrifice.

B. The eucharist

Another communion-sacrifice was the characteristic Christian cult-act, namely the eucharist. This was understood to be communion in the body and blood of Christ, both sharing food in his presence, and feeding on him as the bread of life. In other words, both types of communion-sacrifice have contributed ideas. Notice, however, that it is the body and blood of Christ which are shared. The unique feature of the eucharist as a communion-sacrifice was that the victim was not slaughtered and eaten; rather the sharing of bread and wine was a memorial of Christ's sacrifice. Thus it was intimately connected with the sacrifice of

Christ, and the communion meant participation in the benefits of his redemptive death. In fact, the eucharist refuses to be classified neatly, since it was a sacrifice of praise and thanksgiving offered by the Church in response to redemption in Christ, as well as a re-enactment of his sacrifice and a participation in its benefits. In a sense all types of sacrifice met in this liturgical act, which focused the sacrificial worship of the Church on the sacrificial death of Christ.

SACRIFICES FOR SIN

A. *Baptism*
This was essentially an assimilation of the benefits of Christ's sacrifice, a dying and rising with him (Rom. 6); almsgiving, forgiveness of others, conversion of someone else, charity and penitence; all these were at one time or another regarded as sacrifices able to cleanse from sin.

B. *Spiritual progress*
Progress in Christian virtue, a gradual dying to sin in oneself, was regarded as a spiritual sacrifice for sin.

C. *Martyrdom*
The death of a martyr in imitation of Christ could expiate sin.

All these were ways of dealing with sin, and were referred to as sacrifices at times in Christian literature. But the most important sacrifice for sin was, of course, the death of Christ. Ultimately this really was the one and only sacrifice for sin according to Christian understanding. In the next chapter we shall explore this characteristic Christian feature, bearing in mind in what sense his death was a sacrifice for sin—what type of sin-offering they thought he offered.

4

The sacrifice of Christ

In the last chapter, we have seen how Christians rejected
sacrifice and proclaimed a purely spiritual cult. We have
explored the extent to which this was influenced by the
cultural environment, and how far it was distinctive compared with other contemporary practices and ideas. We
have discovered the wide variety of sacrifices and found
that they were analysable according to the type-analysis
adopted in the first chapter. This led to the conclusion that
the really distinctive feature of the Christian spiritual cult
was the death of Christ, the one and only sacrifice for sin
and the inspiration of all other sacrifices offered by Christians. To that we now turn.

The basic gospel-message (kerygma) of the early mission-
aries contained an appeal for repentance with the promise
of remission of sins.[1] This was associated with the proclamation of the death and resurrection of the Messiah,
Jesus. At a very early stage, these two elements were closely
connected. Already in the New Testament documents, and
particularly the epistles of Paul, we find the idea that the
purpose of the death of Christ was the remission of sins, and
that therefore his death was sacrificial. This was the
beginning of theories about the atoning efficacy of his
sacrificial death.

Two elements in the Jewish background probably
stimulated this development: (i) the idea that the death of
a righteous martyr was expiatory; (ii) the search for
prophecies to account for the totally unexpected idea that
a man who had been crucified was nevertheless God's
Messiah. Since anyone who hung on a tree was cursed in

Deuteronomy (21.23), and therefore cursed by God in his Law, it was utterly paradoxical to claim as Messiah, as God's anointed servant, one who had been subjected to that curse. It is probable that Isaiah 53, the chapter describing the Suffering Servant, contributed to this development, though the evidence is not clear. At least, the early Christians found here a scriptural passage suggesting that 'he was wounded for our transgressions; the Lord has laid on him the iniquity of us all.' This text helped to justify their conviction that the Messiah had died the death of a condemned criminal.

It was inevitable, once the connection was made, that sacrificial language should be used of the death of Christ itself. In the Epistle to the Hebrews, we find the idea that the whole Old Testament sacrificial law had been fulfilled and annulled by the sacrifice of Christ. In fact, all interpretations of Christ's death as sacrificial were at first very closely associated with interpretation of the Old Testament, which was seen as prophecy and foreshadowing of Christ. These interpretations we shall explore first. We call them 'typological' interpretations of Christ's death, because they rest on the idea that a ritual or event in the Old Testament was a 'type' or prophecy, to be exactly fulfilled or paralleled in the Messianic age. We will look at some specific typological themes first, and later the general view that all sacrifices found their fulfilment in the cross.

In the first chapter, brief mention was made of the rituals performed on the Day of Atonement. It was the annual occasion on which special sacrifices for sin were offered, and the High Priest entered the Holy of Holies with the blood of the sin-offerings to purify the very heart of the sanctuary. In the Epistle to the Hebrews, this day is given prominence as a way of understanding the work of Christ. Christ is understood as the true High Priest who entered heaven itself, the true Holy of Holies, and sprinkled his own blood there, performing a single effective act of purification. This purification was accomplished once for all, not repeated daily or annually, and it produced forgiveness not only for ritual infringements and unintentional sins, but cleansed even the consciences of sinful men. Therefore, it fulfilled the old Day of Atonement, and also surpassed and annulled it, being a far more effective means of dealing with sin. Everything was cleansed under the old Law by means of blood rituals, and the author argues that the blood of Christ is a far more efficacious agent for purification, or expiation.

The other ritual characteristic of the Day of Atonement was the scapegoat ceremony, in which the sins of the people were laid on the goat and banished into the desert, to Azazel, the prince of the demons. The Epistle to the Hebrews does not mention this aspect of the Day, but in a later epistle, known as the Epistle of Barnabas, the scapegoat becomes the type of Christ. Christ is depicted as accursed, bearing away the sins of men into the desert. The Old Testament rituals are made to fit the mocking and crucifixion of Christ. This use of the scapegoat idea becomes more and more common in Christian literature, and the point is emphasized that Christ leads away the spiritual hosts of wickedness. In other words, the primitive 'aversion' meaning of the ritual is revived in its new symbolic interpretation.

At different times, then, Christ's saving activity was understood in terms of different aspects of the Day of Atonement ritual. One interpretation clearly understood his sacrifice in an expiatory sense, the other in the sense of aversion.

Passover was another important Jewish festival with certain special characteristics. The application of Passover symbols to the death of Christ is found very early indeed. The earliest reference is in 1 Corinthians 5.7: 'Christ, our Passover, is sacrificed'. In the Gospel of John (19.31), it is clearly implied that Jesus died at the moment when the Passover lambs were being slaughtered in the Temple. These hints were taken up in later Christian literature and developed in greater detail. A carefully worked out parallel was drawn: Israel was delivered from Egypt by God, and the means of escape was the saving blood of the Passover lambs which protected the Israelites from the angel of death. Just so, Christ delivers us from the Egypt of sin and evil, and the means of escape is his own blood, protecting us from the Angel of Death, the devil. Again, what is implied is the primitive 'aversion' type of sacrifice: Christ's blood keeps away evil, death and Satan. Just as Israel was saved from Egypt, so the new Israel, the Church, is saved from sin by the new Passover. This is often described in graphic pictorial language, such as we find in an early Easter sermon by Melito, bishop of Sardis (second century):

> For led as a lamb and slaughtered as a sheep, he ransomed us from the ruin of the world, as from the land of Egypt, and freed us from slavery of the devil, as from the hand of Pharaoh.... This is he who rescued us from slavery to freedom, from darkness to light, from death to life, from oppression to an eternal kingdom, and made us a new priesthood and a chosen people for ever. He is the Passover of our salvation.

In literature of a slightly later period,[2] these ideas were elaborated to absurd detail: allegorical interpretations were given to every minor point, like the bitter herbs, the haste,

the girding of the loins, the wearing of sandals, the carrying of staves, the roasting of the lamb, and so on: but the
central point remained the same, that Christ's death fulfilled the Passover. In an Easter sermon of the fourth century,[3] we read: 'Yesterday the lamb was slaughtered, the
Destroyer passed by and we were protected by the precious
blood of Christ, but today we flee Egypt, and no-one
prevents us feasting with our God. Yesterday we were
crucified with Christ. Today we rise with him.'

Christians celebrated the Passover daily, by feasting 'with
the unleavened bread of sincerity and truth' (1 Cor. 5.8),
'and the bitter herbs of sorrow and repentance'. The
eucharist, too, was a Passover-festival, especially the Easter
eucharist. So the Passover was spiritualized and lived on in
the life and worship of the Christian, as a response to and
memorial of the new Exodus.

So we can see that two ancient Jewish feasts provided
rich symbolical material for interpreting the death of Christ.
The meaning predominant in both was that of an aversion-
sacrifice: the removal of sin, protection from sin, death and
the devil, the escape from slavery to sin and the powers of
evil. In other words the parallels were directly drawn from
the Old Testament but were interpreted in accordance with
primitive rites to keep away evil, rites that had been
sublimated in the Old Testament but remained very much
alive in the contemporary paganism from which most
converts had come.

There was also another powerfully suggestive 'type'
frequently used in the Christian tradition. The Church
from early days regarded itself as being the new Israel,
constituted in a new covenant with God. The new covenant,
a covenant of the spirit, written in the heart, not on tablets
of stone, had been prophesied in Jeremiah (31.31–4). This,
the early Christians believed, was now fulfilled and estab-

lished as a reality by Christ. Paul uses the idea in 2 Corinthians (3.6,14) and Galatians (4.24ff.), stressing the spiritual nature of the covenant which allows the Christian to see the glory of the Lord without the veil with which Moses concealed it (Exod. 34.29ff.). The idea of Christ instituting a new covenant goes back very early in Christian tradition and already, in the accounts of what happened at the Last Supper, the shedding of Christ's blood is associated with the establishment of the new covenant.

One place in early Christian literature where this is brought out in detail is the Epistle to the Hebrews. Moses was the mediator of the old covenant based on the Law engraved on tablets of stone. Christ is the mediator of a new covenant of the spirit (and the whole of Jeremiah 31.31–4 is quoted in ch. 8 of the Epistle to the Hebrews). Moses offered a sacrifice which ratified the old covenant (Exod. 24). This new covenant was likewise established by a sacrifice. So the author draws a typological parallel between the covenant-sacrifice on Mt Sinai and the sacrifice of Christ (Heb. 9.18–21). When he had read all the commandments of the law, Moses took the blood of the sacrificial victims; half of it he threw against the altar, symbolizing God, and the other half over the people, so sealing the blood-covenant between the two parties, God and Israel. By the argument of typology, the blood of Christ was effective in establishing a new and better covenant between God and the New Israel. With his own blood he sprinkled the heavenly altar. The ratification of the new covenant was dependent on the shedding of Christ's blood.

So the Epistle to the Hebrews uses two of these particular typological themes drawn from the Old Testament, the Day of Atonement and the covenant-sacrifice. The parallel is also drawn between Christ's death and the sin-offerings performed daily in the Temple. But these various sacrifices and rituals which the author uses, are not clearly distinguished; they are all confused together in chapters 9 and 10. There are two important points to notice, however: firstly, this Epistle represents the first stage in the process which eventually produced the claim that *all* the sacrificial rituals of the Old Testament had been fulfilled in Christ; and secondly, the understanding of sacrifice is clearly *expiatory*, a point brought out in the author's comments on the rituals he uses.

Christ's death, for the author of the Epistle to the Hebrews, was the fulfilment of the expiatory rites of the Old Testament, and his blood was a means of purification. Outside this Epistle, there is very little about sacrifice as such in the earliest Christian literature. However we find two assumptions, which can only be understood in terms of the sacrificial interpretation of his death. In the first place it was assumed that he died for the forgiveness of sins; but perhaps more important is the assumption that it was his *blood* which had efficacious power to wash away sin. His blood shed on the cross was the fulfilment of the blood rituals of the Old Testament. By the time of the New Testament, the commandment of the law was enough to justify Jewish belief and practice; the Epistle to the Hebrews is itself evidence that the purificatory power of the blood was simply axiomatic: 'under the law, almost everything is purified with blood, and without the shedding of blood, there is no forgiveness of sins'. The sacrificial blood required no further rationale or justification. God had given them the blood upon the altar to make atonement for their souls. Christians just accepted this from the Old Testament scriptures, and saw the blood of Christ as the new God-given means of expiation, God's way of dealing with sin. The application of the blood of Christ was the way of purification. The argument of the Epistle to the Hebrews assumes this atoning principle from the Old Testament.

The blood is the means, and the only means, of obtaining remission and sanctification. The principle was never questioned. There was no difference between the old dispensation and the new on this point. The difference was simply one of degree. This difference of degree is stressed and brought out by the Epistle in two ways:

1. The blood of bulls and goats could only purify pollution of the flesh, whereas Christ's sacrifice could deal with the conscience of the worshippers. The author seems to be referring to the fact that only unintentional infringements of the law could be cleansed by sacrifice, and contrasting the efficacy of Christ's sacrifice for dealing with deliberate sin and disobedience. The blood of Christ had this efficacy because it was the blood of one who was consciously obedient to the will of God.

2. Repeated sacrifices were necessary under the old covenant, but Christ's sacrifice was offered once for all. Once the conscience was cleansed there was no need for further sacrifice.

This basic assumption that the blood of Christ can purify the heart has passed into Christian literature, hymns, and phraseology. It is still used to evoke a response in the believer, and still often does so without explanation. There is an instinct which accepts this idea in spite of its apparent irrationality when examined or questioned. For the early Christians, the Old Testament was sufficient evidence to prove the efficaciousness of blood as a God-given means of expiation. We may require more elucidation, though perhaps its proven power as a symbol evoking instinctive responses, a power discovered not only in evangelical campaigns, but also in Steinbeck's novel, may justify continued use of an apparently irrational and primitive image. Poetry, myths and intuitive symbols are impoverished by too logical an attempt to spell out their meaning. This question will be dealt with more fully in Chapter 6.

However, we should not perhaps leave the matter there without noticing that this interpretation of the meaning of Christ's sacrifice as we find it in the New Testament is not entirely undisputed. Some want to interpret Romans 3.25 and Hebrews 2.17 as meaning 'propitiation' rather than 'expiation'. It is true that the Greek word used is usually translated 'propitiation', and in both cases the general context of the surrounding chapters is an emphasis on God's wrath, his judgement against sin; it is a fearful thing to fall into the hands of the living God, who is a consuming fire (Heb. 10.31; 12.29). For the wrath of God is revealed from heaven against all ungodliness and wickedness of men (Rom. 1.18). Because of these facts, many have argued that the death of Christ is understood in the New Testament as a propitiatory or placatory sacrifice, offered to turn away God's wrath and judgement. But this interpretation does not do full justice to the thought of the passages concerned. In neither case is God's wrath bought off, or bribed away. The cause of his wrath and judgement, that is, sin, is removed, and, as in the Old Testament, it is God alone who can provide the means to do this. It is God alone who can remove, or expiate sin. We have already seen how the Epistle to the Hebrews is based on the Old Testament ideas of purification and expiation, and it is only in this light that Hebrews 2.17 can be properly understood. The sins of the people are the object of Christ's act of expiation. In the case of Romans 3.25, it is clear that the *subject* of the sentence is God: God put forward Christ as an expiation by his blood; propitiation just does not make sense in the context of Paul's statement.

So, as far as the New Testament is concerned, the sacrificial blood of Christ is expiatory, foreshadowed by the sacrifices of the Old Testament, which are fulfilled and annulled by his greater and more efficacious sacrifice. We find no rationale or explanation of how his blood could purify sin, nor was an explanation sought after. However, the New Testament was written in Greek, to pagan converts, and therefore it was only natural that the Jewish concepts lying behind the language of the New Testament should be misunderstood in a new cultural environment, and we can see that this clearly happened. The early Church, once cut from its Jewish roots, lost the Jewish outlook and presuppositions, and very naturally pagan ideas and explanations were imported into the interpretation of both Old and New Testaments. Ideas of 'propitiation' and 'aversion' were introduced to explain how Christ's sacrifice dealt with sin.

This development is clearly seen in the sermons of John Chrysostom on the Epistle to the Hebrews. His name means 'John of the Golden Mouth' and he was the most famous preacher of the early fifth century. When commenting on Hebrews, for much of the time he just accepts that blood purifies, but now and again he feels more explanation is needed and he uses the idea of propitiation to provide this explanation. He accepts very literally what the Epistle says about God's wrath and judgement, especially interpreting it in terms of the Last Judgement; and he clearly understands Christ's sacrifice as a 'buying off' of God's anger. Christ's work consisted in propitiating God, in reconciling us to an angry and hostile God. 'The Son became Mediator between the Father and us. The Father willed not to leave us this inheritance, but was wroth against us, and displeased with us as being estranged from him; he accordingly became mediator between us and him, and won him over.' 'He went up with a sacrifice which had the power to propitiate the Father'.[4] Occasionally Chrysostom feels a bit uncomfortable about this. His predominant message is that God's love is the ground of our salvation; God's love in surrendering his Son for the salvation of the world is compared with Abraham giving up Isaac in sacrifice.[5] Now and again he realizes that the two sides of his preaching do not fit. In one place he corrects himself: it was not the Father who was hostile but the angels![6] But basically in these sermons, we find Christ's sacrifice interpreted in pagan terms as an offering made to propitiate the anger of God.

The fact that Greek converts tended to understand it in this way is borne out by the arguments of more intellectual Christians against this popular interpretation. The Neoplatonists had argued that if God is changeless and perfect, there is no possibility of changing his mind by offering sacrifice. Another corollary of their concept of God was that God could not *really* be angry; for anger is an unseemly passion or emotion, and God, if he is changeless, is also passionless. Men only give way to such emotions because of their animal passions. The ideal was to rise above such things and be changeless like God. It was unworthy of God to think that he could experience the irrational passion of anger. Such was the reasoning followed by many educated Christians. For example, Origen, the most distinguished Christian philosopher of the third century, wrote:

> When we speak of God's wrath, we do not hold that it is an emotional reaction on his part, but something which he uses in order to correct by stern methods those who have committed many terrible sins.[7]

He uses the analogy of a doctor inflicting pain in order to heal, or a schoolmaster chastising in order to improve.

The problem of God's anger is frequently treated in Origen's works, because, of course, there is a great deal in the Old Testament about God's anger and punishment of offenders. Origen and other intellectual Christians had a way of getting round this difficulty. God's revelation, they said, had to be put in earthly terms so that the simple would understand; in fact, however, it points beyond itself to a higher realm. God is not like man, but he chooses to appear like men in order to educate his children. Just as we talk baby-talk to babies—for a baby cannot be expected to understand adult conversation—so we must think God acts with regard to the human race. When you hear of the anger and wrath of God, you must not think that God suffers the emotions of wrath and anger.

> It is a matter of verbal usage for the sake of a child. We put on threatening looks, not because we are angry but for the child's good; if we always show our love and never correct the child, it is the worse for him. It is in this way that God is said to be angry, so as to change and better us.[8]

But of course this argument had another corollary. If God's anger is merely feigned as a means of discipline, then the idea of propitiation is ridiculous, just as it was for the Neoplatonists and other philosophers. A loving Father disciplining his children will cease as soon as the child repents and reforms. There is no mercy in letting him off, unless punishment has had its effect. God deals justice according to a man's present character, and does not deal retribution for past evil once reform has begun.[9] There is no sense in which mercy can be bought or wrath propitiated, on this view of God's dealings with men.

Thus it is clear that as in the Neoplatonists, so in Christian writers, propitiation was re-interpreted. According to Origen, it seems to mean not changing God, but changing man, changing the sinner: Christ goes to the altar in order to 'propitiate me, a sinner'. To convert or reform a man by leading him to repentance is 'to propitiate sin'. It is through Christ's power to improve human beings that his work of 'propitiation' is done.[10] He makes men worthy of the Father's forgiveness, rather than wins round an angry God. Christ was sent by God, so that sinners would forsake their sin and turn to him. Christ is mediator and advocate and the propitiation for the sins of the whole world, because he is God's instrument for converting men from sin and bringing them back to him. The word propitiation is used, but reinterpreted.

What about Christ's sacrifice, then? How is this relevant to the process of reconciling sinners to God? Origen describes sacrifice as a mystery.[11] Nevertheless, in accordance with Christian tradition he draws on the sacrificial language of the Old Testament to describe the death of Christ, and it is possible, through a number of hints, to unearth the interpretation he gave to this idea.

There are occasions when his interpretation appears to be the expiatory one, because he just makes use of scriptural language. The whole of scripture testifies to the fact that sin is purified by sacrificial blood,[12] and Origen does not question the idea. On one occasion he gives a somewhat weird pictorial description of how this works: according to Leviticus, the priests ate the meat of the sin-offering. So, says Origen, Christ, who is priest as well as victim, eats the sins of the people. God is a consuming fire. The God of fire consumes human sins, assumes them, devours them and purges them. Christ took upon himself our sins and, like a fire, he ate and assumed them himself.[13]

Really, however, Origen's thought belongs to another context. We can only appreciate his position if we use the category of 'aversion' sacrifice to elucidate the meaning of Christ's death.

The outlook of Christianity in the ancient world is not easy for us to enter into. In common with much of the religious thought around them the early Christians tended to see the world in dualistic terms,[14] that is, they saw good and evil as two opposed principles, and this idea was personified into a battle between God and the angels on one side, and the devil and the daemons on the other. It is true that this world-view was considerably modified in the total context of Christian doctrine, which stressed that God was ultimately creator of all, as well as ultimately triumphant, and that evil was not really anything, but simply the result of the disobedience of God's creatures. In this way orthodox Christian tradition differed from many contemporary religions, philosophies and heresies, which envisaged an eternal, equally balanced, conflict between good and evil principles. Nevertheless, as far as the practical business of living the Christian life in the world was concerned, Christians saw themselves as engaged in a continuous battle against the hosts of evil; indeed frequently we find the idea that the world is under the dominion of the devil, who is really running it according to his own evil purposes (e.g., John's Gospel, where the devil is called the prince of this world.) All through the early centuries of Christianity, the believer felt himself involved in the warfare between God and devil, good and evil, light and darkness, life and death, righteousness and sin. This battle was typified in the campaign against idolatry, superstition and magic. The martyr felt himself to be at war with all these forces of evil when he died for his faith.

The Christian message was basically a claim that Christ had already achieved the victory and his followers were simply engaging in a 'mopping-up operation'. Christ's work was understood as life deliberately challenging death and conquering it in the resurrection, as good deliberately challenging evil and triumphing, as light deliberately challenging darkness and dispelling it; and each of these pictures could be described mythologically as a cosmic drama in which God was defeating the devil and his angels.

Now Origen was an intellectual who basically saw Christ's work in terms of the revelation of Truth. But nevertheless, his view also fitted into the basic picture outlined just now. As revealer and educator, Christ *conquered* ignorance; as the brightness of God's glory, Christ enlightens the whole world. He makes *war* on his enemies by reason and righteousness, so that what is irrational and wicked is destroyed. The light shines not only on the darkness of men's souls, but has penetrated to where the rulers of this darkness carry on their *struggle* with the race of men.[15] In other words, Origen uses the traditional Christian images of battle and warfare against sin, death and the devil to describe salvation in Christ.

Now this is the context in which we have to understand his ideas about Christ's sacrifice. Chrysostom did not appreciate fully how inconsistent his propitiatory interpretation of Christ's sacrifice was with this prevailing view of what Christ had achieved on the cross. But Origen, over a hundred years before, had struggled with this problem. As we have seen, he was very unhappy with the idea of propitiation on theological grounds; he was groping towards an interpretation of Christ's sacrifice not as propitiation of God, but as *aversion of the devil*. Whenever Origen is seriously seeking an explanation of the traditional sacrifice language he uses, he turns to this basic picture of salvation, that somehow Christ's act on the cross was God's act of overcoming the power of evil !

> The slain lamb of God is made, according to certain mysterious principles, a purification for the whole world ... according to the Father's love to man, he submitted to death purchasing us back by his own blood from the devil who had got us in his power.[16]

The ransom of Christ's sacrificial blood bought off the devil.

Frequently Origen compares this with pagan stories

about men dying for their country to avert plagues and other evils:

> He who was crucified quite recently accepted his death willingly for the human race, like those who died for their country to check epidemics of plague, or famines or stormy seas. For it is probable that in the nature of things there are certain mysteries, causes which are hard for the multitude to understand, which are responsible for the fact that one righteous man dying voluntarily for the community may avert the activities of the evil daemons by expiation, since it is they who bring about plagues or famines or stormy seas or anything similar.[17]

In another passage he uses the same analogy specifically to explain how Christ died for us, and how, since he was the lamb of God, he bore the sins of the world and carried our weaknesses. He goes on:

> How true these stories are or what rational explanation they have, God alone knows, but Jesus was a victim for the whole world, delivering his blood to the prince of this world [i.e. the devil].[18]

So when Origen is pushed to explain Christ's sacrifice for sin he does not turn to propitiation as a rationale. He knows that it was God who *offered* the sacrifice. The sacrifice for sin was a sacrifice of aversion, offered to free mankind from the devil so that man could offer pure worship to God. It may be recalled that this pattern of thought is closely similar to that of Iamblichus. For him, aversion-sacrifices offered escape from the world so as to reach union with the divine.

Origen was able to produce a more consistent theology of Christ's death on the cross. In popular theology, the idea of propitiation was dominant, but it led to inconsistent statements: God is love, God is angry; God sent Christ,

Christ placated God. The idea produced an unhappy picture of the divine Father and Son acting in opposition to one another, and left no real place for the expiatory language of the Bible, though this continued to be used without any real appreciation of its actual import.

Origen was at least consistent: God is love; God acts in Christ to save; Christ offered a sacrifice to save from sin; God in Christ conquered the powers of evil. All this was summed up by understanding Christ's death as an aversion-sacrifice. God offered Christ's blood as a ransom or aversion-sacrifice to buy off the devil and free mankind. This was a spelling out, in the new context of pagan culture, of the biblical idea that God deals with sin through the means of sacrificial blood.

So Christ's sacrifice was understood as a sacrifice for sin, and attempts to translate this idea into pagan culture meant that the sacrifice for sin was understood in a number of different ways which we have been exploring. But it was also claimed that Christ's sacrifice fulfilled the whole of the Old Testament Law. Do we find other types of sacrifice used to interpret Christ's death? A direct answer is not quite possible. The sacrifice of Christ fulfills the Old Testament largely because it is the focus of the whole Christian spiritual cult, but we do find some indications that it was thought of as more than simply a sacrifice for sin. Let us run through the types again.

1. Sacrifices of praise and thanksgiving

In one very real sense, the holocausts were fulfilled in Christ. His sacrifice was a complete self-offering of obedience. His body and soul were offered to God as a gift-sacrifice of worship. This idea is certainly present in the theology of Athanasius, whose defence of Christ's full divinity we mentioned in the first chapter. For him, Christ's

humanity was also of theological importance; it was per-
fected humanity, and when Christ presented himself to
the Father, he offered all humanity in himself as a sacrifice
of perfect obedience.[19] Origen, earlier, had explicitly interpreted the Old Testament holocausts in these terms, as
Christ offering himself on the heavenly altar.[20] Elsewhere
the idea is not clearly expressed, and the sacrifice for sin
is certainly predominant, but it is implied in the fact that
the martyrs were popularly believed to offer themselves
to God as a holocaust, a gift-sacrifice of praise and worship,
and they were also spurred on to this by the thought that
they were acting in *imitation of Christ*.

Christian sacrifices were most often sacrifices of praise
and thanksgiving offered in response to or imitation of the
sacrifice of Christ; Christ's sacrifice was a sacrifice of total
obedience to and glorification of God. Thus, this part of
the Old Testament sacrificial system was fulfilled in Christ.

2. *Sacrifices of communion*

Christ's death on the cross was not thought of as a
communion-sacrifice of the type we have been describing.
But nevertheless, the early Church assumed that he fulfilled
these sacrifices also—in the eucharist. This was a re-
enactment, an effective commemoration of his sacrifice,
and a sacrifice in which his followers partook; the benefits
of his sacrificial death were offered to the Church to be
shared in communion with him and his 'members'. In fact,
as we have seen, the eucharist summed up all Christian
thinking about sacrifice, because it was both a thank-offering
for redemption in Christ and the means of participation in
that redemption.

3. *Sacrifices for sin*

As we have seen, Christ's sacrifice was understood firstly
in the biblical sense of an 'expiatory' sacrifice which dealt
with sin once for all. But in the Gentile context, this was

elucidated sometimes in terms of propitiation, sometimes in terms of aversion-sacrifice.

But if Christ's sacrifice dealt with sin once for all, there was no need for any other sacrifice for sin. This was the argument of the Epistle to the Hebrews. However, it had devastating consequences: a baptized Christian dare not sin again because there is no further forgiveness (Heb. 6). Now this seems false to the whole essence of the Christian gospel, and the Church soon recognized it was utterly impracticable to insist on such a strict standard. So, as we have seen, Christians did offer sacrifices for sin, spiritual sacrifices which they described as sin-offerings, understanding them in one or other of the three senses we have been exploring. But notice how many of these so-called sin-offerings are closely related to the sacrificial death of Christ. Baptism was an entering into the death of Christ; acts of charity and forgiveness, offering oneself in martyrdom, these were done in imitation of Christ; repentance was a prerequisite for assimilating the benefits of Christ's sacrifice, and for progress towards the perfection of Christ. Ideally, everything the Christian did was regarded as a sharing in Christ's sacrifice for sin, taking up arms in his battle against the devil and his angels, adding a contribution to the 'mopping-up operation'. Yet there was a tendency to fall short of this, and to see penance as an attempt to win round an angry deity, a separate act of propitiation whose relation to the sacrifice of Christ was not clarified. It was hard for the ordinary Christian, preacher as well as layman, to cut himself off from the old presuppositions and be perfectly consistent in his thinking. To a very large extent, however, Christ's sacrifice was the central focus of the Christian spiritual cult, and gave it its distinctive character.

PART II

*Some consequences for theology
and the Church today*

5

Atonement and sacrifice

Our historical study has shown us something of the meaning and power of the early Church's appeal to sacrifice as an image of Christ's death on the cross. We can now begin to see how impoverished our thinking has been, and how it may be enriched by the rediscovery of a fuller range of imagery and symbolism. So in this chapter we shall enquire into the consequences of this study for the history of the doctrine of the atonement, and for atonement-theories today. In this discussion we shall assume that the traditional language of sacrifice is still usable, since it is in any case employed in the context of these debates. In the following chapter, we shall turn to the more fundamental question, whether sacrifice can be meaningful today.

It has become customary to distinguish between subjective and objective theories of the atonement. Implied in this distinction is the contrast between the theories produced in medieval times by the near contemporaries, Anselm and Abelard. For the latter, the atoning work of Christ consisted solely in a demonstration of God's eternal love towards mankind in the costly self-giving of his Son on the cross. The cross made no difference to God; atonement was achieved by man's response to that demonstration—it was a 'subjective' human experience. For Anselm, however, the cross was an 'objective' transaction, whereby God was reconciled to sinful man. Something was done on the cross which made a real difference to the status of man in the eyes of God; a change in God's attitude was produced by satisfying the demands of his justice that sin should be punished, by Christ substituting himself for sinful man and receiving the punishment. This was an objective act of atonement, whether or not man recognized it subjectively.

Both these theories are in fact open to considerable objections. However, one or other has tended to dominate thinking on the subject of atonement. Until the late nineteenth century, both Catholic and Protestant theology favoured the objective type of theory and frowned upon Abelard. Abelard appealed to the liberal Protestants, however. As a result, two theological traditions have now developed. Conservatives favour a doctrine of atonement which sees Jesus, the man, bearing punishment in our stead to satisfy the wrath of God. For them this is truly a saving reality, the central core of their faith, the essence of the Christian gospel. Its evangelical appeal cannot be denied. For others, however, such a picture is immoral, repugnant and sub-Christian. God's justice, they say, is hardly maintained by the immoral punishment of an innocent victim instead of the guilty sinner, and it is hardly good Trinitarian theology to envisage a loving Son set over against a wrathful Father as mediator on our behalf. On such grounds, liberals rejected the 'penal substitution' theory in favour of Abelard, and their successors continue to repudiate the notion that the cross could have changed God's attitude towards men. They insist that atonement is an act not done to God, but by God. In retaliation, conservatives have criticized liberals for obscuring the cruciality of the cross, for reducing the objective saving act to a mere subjective experience, for failing to stress the radically new relation of man to God in Christ. Each side has expressed its view with greater degrees of sophistication in order to meet the objections offered, but basically the battle-lines have changed little, except among specialist theologians.

In the early years of this century, the classic histories of the doctrine of atonement were written tendentiously, reflecting a predilection for one or other of these points of view. There was little real attempt to deal sympathetically with the traditional images in terms of their original cultural environment. The sacrifice of Christ was interpreted as necessarily involving the 'objective' type of atonement doctrine; it was understood to imply the offering of suitable compensation to God for the sins of man, as a means of propitiating the wrath of God. Sacrifice was assumed to imply theories of substitution, satisfaction, and propitiation. So the supporters of an objective theory of atonement searched for passages in the New Testament and the Fathers which supported their view, and interpreted all sacrificial references in this light; sacrificial language was seized upon as evidence for the presence of the 'penal substitution' theory, at any rate in germ.[1] A liberal Protestant like Rashdall,[2] however, tended to over-emphasize other images of salvation and, while recognizing the presence of sacrificial imagery, refused to see it as the key to the early Church's understanding of redemption in Christ; it was dismissed as no more than the use of traditional expressions which did not represent the real doctrine held by the authors under discussion. Both sides dismissed as crude aberrations the prevalent pictures of the devil being deceived or paid a ransom by God, failing to see that there must have been something compelling in these pictures for them to be employed by some of the more sophisticated philosophical theologians of the early Church.

Gustaf Aulén's *Christus Victor* led the way to a new appreciation of these images. The notion of a cosmic drama, a battle between the forces of good and evil, was perceived to be the fundamental picture of salvation for the Christians of the early Church, from the New Testament on. A genuine advance was made in understanding the thinking of a period which responded to Christianity as liberation from a world possessed by demons and the powers of evil, and as the final destruction of sorcery and magic, of mental and physical corruption—the destruction even of death itself. It is easy to forget that the notion that supernatural forces were the cause of natural events has only been greeted with general disbelief since the eighteenth century. With Aulén, the old mythological picture of the world was rediscovered and reinstated as the cultural context of the Christian gospel for the early centuries. The death of Christ was a victory over Satan and his angels.

As a result of Aulén's work, the earlier polarization of opinion has to some extent been modified among theologians and historians of doctrine. Increasingly in studies of the atonement, justice has been done to the pre-scientific world-view which was the context of earlier Christian images of salvation, and ransom-theories are now acknowledged and treated sympathetically. However, the traditional understanding of sacrifice has persisted, even in the work of Aulén, who assumes that sacrifice is naturally regarded as offered to God, while ransom is the price paid by God to redeem mankind from bondage to the devil. But how could the death of Christ be both a sacrifice to God and a ransom to the devil? If the conquest of the devil was the basic requirement for dealing with evil, why should sacrifice to God be necessary? How could a ransom offered by God be also a sacrifice offered to God? Was Aulén's distinction at all valid?

Aulén went on to argue that the two images overlapped, the argument being that since the early Church ultimately believed in the sovereignty of God over evil, ransoming the devil could be, and in fact was, regarded as a divine act of self-reconciliation. This observation is certainly accurate with regard to Athanasius, and we shall return to clarify this point at a later stage. But I am sure that this total conspectus was not consciously present in the minds of most

Christians of the early Church. Our study has shown that the coincidence of ransom and sacrifice language is due not to any overall theological position, but to the vast range of possible understandings of sacrifice. It not only implied an offering made to propitiate God; indeed the sacrificial imagery could just as easily be understood in terms of God averting the devil or God expiating human sin. In particular, our exposition of Origen's understanding of sacrifice shows that Aulén's distinction between sacrifice offered to God and ransom offered to the devil is not valid; both sacrifice and ransom were, for Origen, part of the cosmic drama of victory over the opposing evil powers, accomplished by God himself on behalf of the human race.

Nevertheless, with this modification that there was no inherent distinction between the images of sacrifice and ransom, our explorations have confirmed the value of Aulén's insights from a historical point of view. We have to recognize that in understanding atonement, there have been more than the two polarized viewpoints with which we opened our discussion in this chapter, and no history of the doctrine can be fair which denigrates what Aulén called the 'classic' theory of atonement. The recognition of this has already had a profound effect on more recent studies of atonement. For F. W. Dillistone this view becomes one of a number of ways in which Christians have understood the work of Christ, and these he sets out to explore and interpret in his book *The Christian Understanding of Atonement*. Its importance in the Fathers is fully recognized also by F. R. Barry in his study, *The Atonement*, and in a later chapter he takes it up as a fruitful line of exploration in interpreting atonement for today. Earlier, H. A. Hodges, in *The Pattern of Atonement*, had followed a brilliant critique of the traditional theory of satisfaction and substitution with a restatement, in counterbalance to it, of this very theory. This is not to say that the concept of warfare with a personal devil is advocated. Clearly some 'demythologizing' is necessary. However, atonement is treated in terms of the conflict between good and evil in the creation, with an insistence that it comes *from* God, rather than being satisfaction offered *to* God. The intention and result of atonement are described as the ending of man's enslavement to false ideologies and uncontrollable psychological forces. Atonement becomes relevant to the destructive powers of the 'system', the political and economic forces which are more than the sum total of the individuals involved or their conscious intentions, the heredity and environment which so often turn good things to evil purposes. One real advantage of approaching the problem of atonement along the lines of the classic theory is that instead of being limited to the riddance of one type of guilt feeling, the salvation brought by Christ is shown to be relevant to all forms of alienation, all problems of human failure—indeed the total nexus of evil in the world. Another advantage is that emphasis is placed on the saving action of God and a division between the persons of the Godhead, Father and Son, is avoided. One result of our study is certainly to spotlight again the key role of ransom imagery in the thinking of the early Church, and again to direct attention to alternative possibilities to the traditional party-lines.

More important, however, is the rediscovery of the central importance of sacrificial imagery in the early Church's thinking. For the early Church, sacrifice was an image which could focus with peculiar intensity the full significance of the life and death of Christ for the salvation of the world; it played a vital part in the belief and worship of Christians of that period. It cannot be dismissed as alien or peripheral to the real thought of the authors on the atonement issue. It is false to the evidence to relegate it to the sidelines. It is equally false to the evidence to assume that every sacrificial image implies a particular theory of atonement. To continue the debate between two inadequate theories of atonement is to be blind to the fact that the use of sacrificial imagery did not always imply the 'penal substitution' theory in germ. It could mean God's act of expiating sin as well as man's act of propitiating God. It could imply aversion of the evil powers, and so coincide with the view that atonement was the victory of the forces of good over the powers of evil.

Indeed, Aulén's discovery of the overriding importance of this view in the early Church should not lull us into an over-simplifying picture of the doctrine of atonement in the early Church. Just because we have found such a range of possible references in sacrificial imagery, the tensions and dilemmas of atonement theory are unlikely to be resolved simply by an appeal to this imagery—indeed, they are more likely to be highlighted. It is a gain to see that propitiatory sacrifice is but one type, but the rich and varied range of meaning implicit in the imagery leaves open the possibility of unsystematic thinking and unresolved paradoxes. There is a fundamental inconsistency between thinking of Christ's sacrifice as an act performed by God to avert the devil and thinking of it as an offering made to God to appease his wrath. Both of these, however, were present in the thinking of the early Church, and for John Chrysostom the inconsistency was never resolved, though he occasionally felt some embarrassment about it. The vast majority of Christians in the early Church, as indeed the majority today, adopted traditional patterns of imagery and language without any real appreciation of the contradictions inherent in them. God is love; God is angry. God is ultimately responsible for everything; the devil is responsible for evil. God sent his Son to overcome evil; God was placated by his Son's sacrifice. Sacrificial imagery could be used to represent either of these attitudes in a forceful and compelling way.

It is noticeable that in speaking of the expressions for atonement used by the Fathers, we repeatedly describe them as imagery. Generally speaking, the standard estimate of the Fathers is correct: they used a vast range of imaginative symbols and failed to produce a doctrine or theory of atonement, while carrying definitions of the Trinity to extreme niceties. Yet this does not mean that they were indifferent to the fact of atonement or to its expression. Indeed, the intensity of the doctrinal conflicts reflected their search for theological definitions which could do justice to their understanding of the gospel of redemption. Their very refusal to over-simplify or confine their beliefs to definitive categories reflects some appreciation of the complexity of the issues involved. In any case, there were certainly some who did not try to avoid grappling with the problems inherent in the images used, as we can see in the case of Origen, for example, and later Gregory of Nyssa. By stressing God's redemptive love in a more thorough-going way, and rationalizing away his wrath, these two produced a theory of atonement which was on the face of it more self-consistent, avoiding the notion of propitiation and stressing God's victory over evil. The idea of God offering a ransom to the devil to free mankind from slavery was expressed in vivid imagery which has proved repugnant to later generations of Christians, but we should not for this reason be blind to the significance of what they were saying. Out of a deep awareness of God's love and goodness towards mankind, they produced an interpretation of the images which at first sight appears more rational and consistent. Yet it raises other difficult tensions; for the same deep awareness of God's love and goodness meant that they were unwilling to attribute to God any responsibility for evil. Their convictions about the sovereign love of the

Creator led them to argue for the unreality and non-existence of evil, a view hardly compatible with their understanding of atonement as its conquest and destruction. Furthermore, they were not afraid to speak of Christ's sacrifice as an offering to God as well as to the devil, without resolving the paradoxes involved in such a view.

When Gregory of Nazianzus rejected the notion of payment to the devil and appealed to the mystery of the 'economy' (by which he meant something like 'God's self-adaptation for the purposes of the divine plan'), he was admitting the difficulty of dealing with these images at a rational level. Nevertheless, it seems to me that the tensions and paradoxes implicit in the thought and language of the Greek Fathers had been to a fair extent resolved in the work of Athanasius, whose *De Incarnatione* was a major attempt to present the Christian gospel in a systematic way. He recognized that a straightforward conflict between good and evil did not do justice to the situation, even though it reflected a profound appreciation that atonement was an act of God. It was necessary, in spite of the difficulties, to allow a measure of responsibility to God for the mess from which mankind needed salvation. So he suggested that evil and disobedience had produced an intolerable tension between God's goodness and his integrity. It put God into a dilemma. It was unthinkable that he should go back on his word and man, having transgressed, should not die; God could not falsify himself. But it was not worthy of his goodness that his creature should perish; it would have been better never to have created him. Somehow God's integrity had to be salvaged while the demands of his love were met. The sacrifice of Christ was the solution to this dilemma; it was a sort of 'self-propitiation' offered by God to God to make atonement for the existence of evil in his universe. It took the form of paying the debt to death; it could be expressed in traditional terms as paying a ransom to the devil; but Aulén was right in pointing here to an underlying doctrine of self-reconciliation.[3]

In a new history of the doctrine of atonement, then, justice must be done to the central importance of sacrificial imagery in the thinking of the early Church, and to the significance of the work of Athanasius in resolving the tensions inherent in early Christian thinking about atonement. As a consequence, one may hope that the persistent polarization of opinion about atonement may be mitigated. There is much in the 'penal substitution' theory which comes near to the Athanasian picture, for it seeks to resolve the tension between God's justice and his mercy, his holiness and his love. We must begin to recognize that a simple clear-cut pattern fails to be sensitive to the ambiguous and elusive character of the relationship between God and the evil in his creation. Atonement means a conviction that God has somehow dealt with evil, with sin, with rebellion. Perhaps the nearest we can get to expressing this is to say that on the cross, God in Christ entered into the suffering, the evil, and the sin of his world; he entered the darkness and transformed it into light, into blazing glory. He took responsibility for the existence of evil in his creation; he bore the pain of it and the guilt of it; he accepted its consequences into himself, and in his love reconciled his holiness to a sinful and corrupt humanity, justifying the ungodly, accepting man just as he is:

> Here was no overlooking of guilt or trifling with forgiveness; no external treatment of sin, but a radical, a drastic, a passionate and absolutely final acceptance of the terrible situation, and an absorption by the very God himself of the fatal disease so as to neutralize it effectively.[4]

This is perhaps poetic understanding or the insight of faith, rather than a theological conclusion based on logical argument. It is a conclusion, however, that does justice to the objective character of the atoning act, while avoiding the moral and theological difficulties of the Anselmian type of theory. The cross was no mere demonstration of God's love; it was a very costly act of 'self-propitiation'. And if the language we use to describe it is poetic, anthropomorphic or 'mythological', we shall see in the following chapter that it will be the more powerful for that very reason.

The first consequence of our study, then, must be to extend our understanding of the meaning of sacrifice when applied to the death of Christ and so open up wider perspectives on the whole matter of atonement theory. Our constructive conclusions about the atonement have arisen directly out of a subtler understanding of sacrifice as an act not only offered to God, but an act performed by God himself. But our discoveries about the early Church must press us on further. For in that cultural setting, sacrificial language was used not only of the death of Christ, but of large areas of Christian worship and practice. Thus the imagery refused to allow them to fall into the trap of divorcing atonement theory from faith and response. The atonement may not be 'merely' subjective, but it must be subjective as well as objective. The evil in us is not met and conquered by an act external to us. The objective act makes our acceptance and redemption possible, but it must meet with response; it must effect a transformation in the believer. For the early Church, there was an intimate relationship between the sacrifice of Christ and the sacrificial worship and service of the Church; there was an indissoluble bond linking Christ's sacrifice of obedience to the spiritual sacrifices of the saint and the martyr. For the sacrifice of Christ was itself more than an atoning sacrifice; it was a sacrifice of worship and obedience. There were two sides to his sacrificial act, the removal of evil and sin by God, and the offering of perfect homage by man.

The recognition of the importance of this for the early Church must have a profound effect on our narrow attitudes to atonement theory. The context in which we regard the sacrifice of Christ should be that of the worshipping community, and its full significance is only to be grasped when that context is fully recognized. Sacrifice is properly treated as cult-language, not the language of law-courts and judgements; in this context, Christ's act is seen as a sacrifice in which Christians have to partake in order to receive its benefits. Such an appreciation of the context of atonement will make a difference to our understanding of the eucharistic sacrifice, and the whole range of Christian response to God's saving act in Christ. The sacrifice of Christ becomes the focus of a complete spiritual cult.

The sacrifice of Christ was God's act of salvation, a sacrifice offered by God to expiate sin, to avert the devil, and reconcile God with himself; to this Christians responded with sacrifices of praise and thanksgiving. But that is only the simplest understanding of the relationship between his sacrifice and that of believers. For the sacrifice of Christ was a sacrifice of perfect obedience to God; it was itself perfect homage, a sacrifice of praise and thanksgiving offered by man, a sacrifice which men may imitate and into which they may be drawn. It was a sacrifice offered for men, on their behalf; it was an objective act of sacrifice, but an act with which men must identify themselves in response. Atonement is at least a demonstration of God's love to which response has to be made. It has a subjective element as well as an objective one. But it is more than simply response, for it is only realizable in mankind when men respond by making their own self-sacrifice, imitating his sacrifice, dying with him in repentance and baptism, entering into his sufferings and his perfect obedience, submitting even to martyrdom. The sacrificial language of the early Church represented not merely response to, but participation in the sacrifice of Christ. Worship, service, and atonement were inseparable. The same should be true for the Church today.

To some people this emphasis on the response of the Christian may seem to undermine the doctrine of justification by faith. It may be felt that it is dangerous to speak of the need for 'works' like almsgiving, vows of poverty, saying masses or dying as a martyr, if atonement is to be made effective. But this is to misunderstand the whole force of what is being said. We are saved by faith surely because God has done for us what we could not do for ourselves. Only God has the power to remould warped consciences and free the mind from slavery to its favourite psychological sicknesses and pet sins. Man cannot free himself from his follies and idols simply by wanting to or trying hard. We are justified by faith, not because Jesus Christ and his Father have patched up an agreement whereby our sins are to be ignored, but because by faith in Christ we are accepted, sinners as we are, and enabled to identify with his perfection, to share in his perfect sacrifice of praise and obedience. We are redeemed from corruption and re-created in newness of life. Worship, service and atonement are inseparable.

The traditional patterns of atonement theory have always been highly individualistic, and so far our exposition has tended to fall into this same mould. We think of atonement as affecting each individual soul, of each individual believer responding to God's action in Christ. However, for the Fathers of the Greek Church, with whom we have mainly been concerned, the whole of humanity was summed up in the manhood of Christ. This is a difficult notion for us to grasp, but a 'corporate' understanding of Christ's manhood is already present in Paul, where Christ as the Second Adam enables mankind to be a 'new creation' in himself. Our thinking tends to be incurably individualistic, and our study may be a valuable corrective in this direction too. Atonement is not simply the individual standing before the tribunal of God. It is concerned with all forms of evil in the world, and a good deal of evil is the result of human failure to create community. When we see the sacrifice of Christ in the context of the worshipping community, we have a new perspective. The believing Christian does not simply enter as an individual into a moral and emotional identification with Christ at a purely subjective level, but he takes his place in a community which is, or at least attempts to be, the body of Christ on earth. This community enters into and continues the saving activity of Christ, and responds to it by offering spiritual sacrifices of worship through him. In this way, mankind within the body of Christ is being restored to perfect community among men and perfect communion with God. The unity of Christ and the Christian is objectively expressed in the communal life of the Church. Christ's work of atonement can only be accomplished fully in that context, and a proper understanding of it cannot be reached in isolation from consideration of the Church's life, service and worship. Christ and his Church are mutually involved in sacrificial activity.

The eucharist sums all this up. In debate and controversy about the eucharist, the variety of meanings of sacrifice has long been observed, and the old battle as to whether the eucharist is a sacrifice or not has been somewhat alleviated by this recognition. The Protestant tradition has been prepared to admit that the eucharist is a sacrifice in the sense that it is an offering of worship, praise and thanksgiving, an assumption that was integral to the thinking of the early Church. The eucharist is at least a 'first-fruit' offering, a harvest-festival, in which praise and thanks for creation are offered; it is also a sacrifice of thanksgiving for our redemption in Christ. It is the relationship between the eucharist and the sacrifice of Christ which has remained a bone of contention. Here debate and controversy have been vitiated by the old narrow concept of sacrifice. Whether regarded as a 'mere remembrance' or as a 'repetition' of the sacrifice of Christ, it has been associated with propitiatory ideas, with offering up something to compensate for the sins of man. It has been regarded as a re-enactment of, or remembrance of, the transaction at Calvary; it has been performed in the belief that its repetition is effective in propitiating God, or received in the belief that the benefits of the once-for-all transaction are made available to the individual through the bread and wine. So the debate has focused on whether the transaction was once-for-all, or whether it is effectively repeated at each offering of the eucharist. The consequences of this controversy have been parallel debates about priesthood, the Catholic tradition insisting that the priest is one set apart to sacrifice the Mass on behalf of the people.

Much of this strife has been the result of failure to see both atonement and eucharist in the context of the worshipping community united with Christ as his body on earth. For the early Fathers, the sacrifice of the eucharist was the culmination of a total spiritual cult involving the whole life and service of Christians. It was the self-offering of Christians in response to the self-offering of Christ—and not simply a response, for this was not *another* offering but the same offering as his, redeemed humanity united in offering homage to God. It was not simply the individual before God, nor the priest offering a sacrifice for the people. It was Christ and his Church offering together; it was a sacrifice of communion, a fellowship-meal of the new community, uniting the partakers in worship, faith, and service. Thus it was neither a new offering to God, nor simply receiving the benefits of the offering of Christ, but rather the realization of God's act of atonement in and for the worshippers.

In this chapter, the aim has been to show how the results of our historical study might affect and modify present-day discussions. The suggestion is that a fresh appreciation of the fact that sacrifice had a variety of meanings in the early Church could do much to resolve the traditional lines of conflict in relation not only to the eucharistic sacrifice, but also to atonement. It might release us all from the narrow confines of hostile and mutually suspicious parties, if we could only open our minds and withdraw the emotions invested in restrictive presuppositions and assumptions. It could help us to recognize the complexity of the problems and bring us to a more humble, yet more profound appreciation of the mystery of what God has done for us in Christ. As such it could be a positive contribution to ecumenical discussions.

6

Can sacrifice mean anything to us?

In the last chapter we entered into the traditional debates
about the meaning of Christ's sacrifice on the cross, on the
assumption that such an approach was still meaningful and
viable. Some, however, may be tempted to think that the
whole discussion was remote and academic, perhaps of use
to ecumenically-minded clerics, but hardly relevant to the
average intelligent churchgoer. How is all this theological
controversy to be preached? What relevance has Christ's
sacrificial death, or the spiritual sacrifices of the Church, to
the lives of twentieth-century Christians?

This is an important question, if only because one important emphasis in our historical study has been the
links between Christian expression and contemporary
culture in the Graeco-Roman world. The language of sacrifice was so powerful precisely because it was absolutely basic
to all religious expectations in the surrounding environment. It was one of those unquestioned assumptions, a
presupposition that needed no exposition. Indeed apologetic required explanation of the Christians' refusal to
offer sacrifice in a literal way. The use of sacrificial language
in a symbolical way was inevitable in such a situation.

It is the power of the symbolism that is so important.
Religious language has its life in symbols, not cold theological definitions or logical arguments. Religion uses metaphor, imagery and symbol to convey its truth, like poetry
and art. Myths and symbols are the language of creative
expression. When the symbols cease to have an immediate
impact, then interpretation and rationalization begin, with
an inevitable tendency to narrow the reference and reduce
the overtones to a consistent philosophy. Thus the life of

the symbol enters its terminal phase.

> A true symbol always possesses overtones, so that its
> full significance cannot be grasped intellectually, at least
> immediately. If it becomes definable in rational terms,
> it is no longer a living symbol ... For St Paul and for the
> early mystics, the cross stood for something which could
> not be clearly defined, but which was of immense im-
> portance. As time went on, the cross no longer bore the
> same significance.[1]

The symbol which had been 'pregnant with meaning' and
could not be 'sharply defined in purely intellectual terms'
was understood by means of analogies or rationalizations
which could only narrow and restrict its full significance. In
the previous chapter, we were coping with the results of
the death of sacrificial symbols and images which had been
brought about by a restriction and rationalization of their
reference. The immediacy of response to the sacrifice of
Christ was obscured by cold-blooded explication and
analysis of the rational content of the symbol.

Yet is it inevitable that explanation and elucidation
should impoverish? Our historical study surely could serve
to justify the claim that the spiritualization or rationalization of sacrificial worship was a positive religious advance
which Christianity pioneered for European civilization. The
beginnings of conscious inquiry about sacrifice produced
healthy denials of crude misconceptions, an awareness of
deeper levels of spiritual insight, a more profound concept
of the nature of the divine. The first definition of sacrifice
was produced when literal sacrifice was a thing of the past,
but no one could call it a sterile or narrow conception: 'a
true sacrifice is any act that is done in order that we may
cleave in holy union to God'.[2] The use of sacrificial language
had its dangers without this rationalizing and deepening.
We have seen how Christianity reflected the cultural con-

text in its pursuit of a profounder understanding of sacrifice in all its types. It is not rationalization that kills a symbol, but restriction, confinement to a single definition, and conscious effacement of its manifold overtones. Description and elucidation can serve to show the richness of the images.

We are nevertheless confronted with a problem. For the early Church, sacrificial imagery was powerful and inevitable. For us, it is by no means inevitable, and far from powerful—indeed, it is more often an offence and a stumbling-block. If we are to learn from the early Church, we probably need to find alternative images or symbols from our own culture, with a similar immediate impact. That is no easy task, however, and I do not claim to be able to produce a solution to that difficulty. What I want to suggest in this chapter is that whatever our immediate reaction to the language of sacrifice, the realities which were expressed in this imagery are still relevant in the life of the Church today, and whether or not we can find an alternative symbolism, we still need to express the same range of ideas as our predecessors once expressed through sacrificial symbols. Indeed, we may have to consider the possibility that a courageous and imaginative revival of the old symbolism may be the only way of bringing the realities to the consciousness of this generation. But if revival is the only way, then it must be informed by a proper appreciation of the wider implications, the layers of meanings and overtones, the variety of significances of the symbols we try to use. Interpretation must be an enriching, not an impoverishing task.

This is not to say that we should try an obscurantist 'back-to-the-early-Church' movement and accept the whole package without criticism. There are many hindrances to this. For example, a straightforward acceptance of the notions of the early Church about the fulfilment of Old Testament sacrifices on the cross would be difficult for the majority of thinking Christians, except for perhaps the most conservative believers. A revival of sacrificial imagery needs to be aware of the basic religious impulses of mankind from which the rituals sprang and to which sacrificial imagery has continued to appeal down the ages. So we need to search out the areas of human experience which have been illuminated or resolved by the practice of sacrifice, or substitutes for it.

The task of revival is perhaps not as difficult as it might seem at first sight. The fact that ancient myths and symbols can still catch the imagination is proved by the 'cult' of J. R. R. Tolkien's novels,[3] depicting a fantasy world in which pure good finally triumphs over unmitigated evil, and employing the traditional motifs of European folk-lore and heroic sagas. As far as sacrifice is concerned, we have already been able to make use of two modern novels which provide dramatic presentations of the emotions and impulses directed into sacrificial practices. Anthropological studies have revealed the universality of sacrifice among primitive peoples as a response to life and to their environment. Sacrificial rituals and the myths and symbols of religion have provided psychologists with insight into the workings of the human consciousness—indeed, Jung concluded that the only appropriate answer to severe emotional problems was to be found in symbols of this kind.[4] It is for reasons like this that novelists have been able to recreate for us dramatic situations in which we can appreciate the full force of sacrifice as a focus of human drives and emotions. For the same reasons the traditional Christian language of sacrifice could be made to live again if it could be released from the confines of restricting and formal definitions and be allowed to speak as poetic symbolism. Literature and drama can provide us with examples of how sacrificial symbolism can live again for us.

A BBC 1 production in the *Menace* series[5] provides a

104

useful illustration. Half-a-dozen middle-aged executives are sent to an Outdoor Centre and subjected to a gruelling week of physical exercises. They start with gymnastics, climbing up ropes and over obstacles; they go on to crossing roaring rivers, climbing vertical cliffs, and joining in long-distance treks over snow-covered mountain areas, the idea being to test their reactions under stress. The youngest and fittest of the group bounces in at the start and introduces himself as in the running for a directorship, which he is almost certain to get since he is the boss's son-in-law. At the first gathering for dinner, however, it is revealed publicly that they are all from different branches of the same firm and all in competition for the same job. Out of their stunned reaction is born a hostility to the boss's son-in-law which gradually affects them all. They feel he has an unfair advantage, and as he consistently shows up better in all the exercises, their hostility grows. He is subjected to petty spiteful tricks. He succeeds in alienating the entire group, and becomes 'accident-prone'. It was not for nothing that the director of the Outdoor Centre began to get alarmed. The accidents were unlikely to be accidents: the rope held safely for all the others, but broke as *he* crossed the river, sweeping him downstream in a dangerous current; on a perfectly safe, clean cliff, a boulder came loose and descended, striking *him* on the shoulder. The more he helped out others in difficulties, the more enthusiasm he displayed, the more the bitterness increased. Nor was the situation helped by the favouritism shown him by the director's wife. The tense atmosphere grew until eventually, by mutual consent, an emergency was developed in which he was 'accidentally' killed—some accident!—for we watched the boots pressed on his hands and into his face to prevent him from climbing to safety! The fears and aggressions of each individual had been fed in the group situation and focused on one member of it, until collectively they did something to which no single individual could have brought himself. The climax of the play was the revelation that he had been sent merely as a catalyst, and was the one person there who had no hope of the job at all.

The play was called *Judas Goat*, and it expressed dramatically the sort of thing observed among group therapists, that groups have an emotional dynamic of their own, which is greater than that of the individuals of which they are made up. It illustrated the tendency for fear, frustration, insecurity, and compensating aggressions to be magnified in a group and focused on a 'scapegoat', which is then banished from the group. Undoubtedly this sort of thing lies behind the story of Jonah being cast into the sea to remove ill-luck from the ship in which he was travelling, though in the Old Testament the story is retold in terms of God's will and providence. Now of course, the use of scapegoat language in this sort of context is metaphorical. But metaphors can express nothing if there is no parallel involved. There is undoubtedly a sense in which the scapegoat-rituals of the Old Testament and among other primitive peoples have a parallel in the making of one individual into a 'scapegoat' in a group situation. In both cases, fears and aggressions and the associated guilt-feelings are projected on to the 'scapegoat', who is driven out of the group so as to remove the disruptive influence of these emotions. In the case of the group observed by modern psychotherapists, the 'scapegoating' is unconscious, hostile, and dangerous to the community. In the case of the old rituals, a surrogate was provided; the situation was to some extent consciously accepted and resolved by ritualizing it or dramatizing it. Thus the guilt caused by the presence of disruptive aggressions and fears was cancelled and the community was able to survive.[6]

The conclusion suggested by this example is that human beings are still driven by the same emotional responses today as ever, but modern life has obliterated the safety-valve of ritualism. In the respectability of modern society, we try to deny our aggressions, guilts, and fears. In suppressing them, we find unconscious outlets. It is true that not many of us have been involved in an 'accidental' murder, but probably all of us have recollections of groups in which one person has been forced to 'carry the can' or accept the blame beyond all that is reasonable or justifiable. An unpopular sister in a hospital ward may be the focus of the anxieties and frustrations of the patients, who consequently treat her with hostility and aggression, blaming her for every discomfort, perhaps even for failure to recover. She is made a 'scapegoat'. There is surely a sense in which the recognition and acceptance of these emotions, and their 'catharsis' or purification by ritual means, were a more healthy and constructive approach. The primitive rituals had a function to perform in society, and symbols drawn from them may be relevant to understanding our own situation today.

Other things certainly perform a parallel function in our society, thus replacing the primitive rituals. In drama, novels, art, and music—not to mention competitive sport —people today experience their emotions, their aggressions and guilts in ritualized and harmless forms. Spectators identify 'our' team, and feel hostility and fear towards 'the others'. Music evokes the whole gamut of emotion as well as aesthetic appreciation. Violence on TV, far from encouraging violence in society, may in fact be one of our ritual safety-valves, allowing people to experience their aggression harmlessly; the cartoon *Tom and Jerry* is a well-loved example of extreme violence in a harmless form because it is entirely and obviously fantasy.[7] Drama, in particular, has always had a ritual function. Modern drama developed out of the religious mystery-play; the great drama of ancient Greece likewise developed out of a religious ritual, and always remained a religious festival. The philosopher, Aristotle, recognized in drama the means of experiencing and dealing with extreme emotions; indeed, he used the word 'catharsis' of the purging effect of dramatic presentations on the audience. Actual participation in the drama or dramatic liturgy is not necessary, as long as there is *emotional* participation—in other words, the viewers identify with the feelings of the actors or players, and experience their passions in doing so. The non-rational, indeed 'bestial' side of human nature is accepted and dealt with by sharing in the actions and passions of a representative figure.

One cannot help feeling that the cross of Christ could be, and indeed still is for many people, an effective symbol in this regard. He is the one who was 'scapegoated', the one on whom the aggressions and frustrations of his contemporaries were focused. It is simply not true that men respond to love and selflessness when they see it. People reacted then as they would still. Jesus' attitude broke too many social conventions; it upset the *status quo*; it conjured up visions of disorder and chaos. 'People should be kept in their place,' they felt; 'the old standards should be maintained. This consorting with publicans and sinners is dangerous. This breaking of the traditional rules is the thin end of the wedge. Something must be done in the name of God and the present religious and political set-up.' So Jesus becomes the focus of hostility. They try to trap him and catch him out; they trick him into situations which will bring his condemnation. They patch up a charge near enough the truth to get him condemned in the Roman courts: he is undermining the Empire by preaching about the kingdom of God. Ironically enough, Pilate is induced to release a real guerilla and condemn this mock-prince, Jesus. So Jesus becomes the 'scapegoat', the focus of hostility, because he brought insecurity and anxiety. He is cast out of the community, he is murdered because of their frustrations and fears. In this historical sense, he is like the 'Judas Goat', and suffers because of the cruel and dangerous passions of man. Yet the situation is redeemed because he consciously accepted men for what they were, deliberately 'set his face to go to Jerusalem', and accepted into himself all that men could do to him. He took up the role of martyr, believing that by so doing he could bear and expiate the sins of the people. For us, the story of his passion can be a dramatic or ritual way of dealing with the emotions we would like to repress and deny. The scapegoat ritual made the people conscious of their sin, as well as providing a means of dealing with it. In the same way, the drama of the passion can make us conscious of our aggression and guilt, showing us up for what we really are, while at the same time providing a symbolic way of dissolving the destructive effect of our emotions. By accepting their consequences into himself, Jesus Christ enables us to accept them and to cope with our guilt and inadequacy.

To some extent, the 'cathartic' effect of the passion-story can be rationalized. We see ourselves being accepted for what we really are. It is a presupposition of modern psychotherapy and child psychology that a person needs a relationship in which he is unconditionally accepted, faults and all, in order to be able to accept himself, to become a mature, integrated personality.[8] The cross can be seen as a costly demonstration of that acceptance. But in the end, this rationalization of the drama does not convey its full significance. Our sense that the ritual deals with our guilt and inadequacy is instinctive and immediate, rather than resting on psychological or rationalizing explanations. The symbol is more than any explication of it. We feel a sense of relief and peace in seeing him accepting the situation in all its appalling tragedy. We know the healing effect of weeping as a great tragic drama is presented. In the same way, the cross can have a dramatic effect upon us, healing us by summoning up tears of repentance and joy.

This is one example of the kind of thing I mean by saying that the traditional Christian language of sacrifice could be made to live again if it could be released from the confines of formal theological definitions and be allowed to speak as poetic symbolism. The scapegoat ritual was a primitive cult practice of the same general type as the rites of sacrifice, and we have seen that it can be used metaphorically and symbolically to produce a suggestive and dramatic account of the significance of the cross. We shall return to many of these themes later when we explore the relevance of sin-offerings to the understanding of Christ's death on the cross. Meanwhile we need to ask whether similar significance can be found more generally in the whole area of sacrifice language which we have been exploring.

We should now be able to see that our failure to understand the implications of sacrifice is largely due to the very process of development in ideas which we traced in our historical study. With a higher concept of God, and a greater sense of his sovereignty, people began to see that he could not need or want anything. So the idea of offering something to God was overshadowed by stress on the giver giving up something—fasting became a sacrifice, and sacrifice to us means to deny ourselves something we desire or care about—giving up sweets in Lent, for instance, or sacrificing our particular interests to those of the nation as a whole.

If we are to appreciate the meaning of sacrifice in religion, and in Christianity in particular, we need to forget our idiomatic use of the word and return to the idea of offering or sanctifying; we need to remember that sacrifice comes from cults, from rituals of worship. It seems to me that sacrifice, properly understood, is integral to a religious response to the universe.

Now if this is so, it is not surprising that sacrificial language has lived on in Christian traditions, even though the practice of sacrificial rites ceased long ago; our study of the meaning of sacrifice has not been in vain if it has helped us to appreciate again the real implications of the traditional language we use. But can we go further and 'demythologize' the various types of sacrifice, can we uncover the layers of meaning in the symbols, so that we can see that they remain active in the Church and relevant today? I believe we can; and this will not simply be salvaging as much as possible from primitive ideas which we have in fact outgrown, but a rediscovery of fundamental religious responses at a deep instinctual level. If this is so, our endeavours will be rewarded by an enriched understanding of our religious experience and the language in which we, by custom, express it.

There is, of course, a considerable difference between a primitive tribe sacrificing to mysterious powers around it in nature and the Christian worship of God conceived as the Creator and sovereign of the universe. But there is one thing in common: sacrifice, material or spiritual, is a reaction to the unseen power believed to be hidden in the world about us, and the different types of sacrifice can be seen as expressions of different reactions to the environment. Yet again, it will be useful to think through the various types we have traced.

1

SACRIFICES OF WORSHIP AND THANKSGIVING

Sacrifices of this kind clearly arose from the recognition that even if man sowed the seed, he did not make it grow;

even if he cares for the sheep, he cannot produce the wool. Gift-sacrifices were a natural reaction to prosperity and plenty. Primitive man was only too conscious of his dependence.

Perhaps the clearest distinction between the man who feels a need for religion and the one who does not, is the fact that in the former a sense of inadequacy predominates, while the other has a greater sense of *self*-sufficiency and independence. This is surely one key to the loss of religious faith in the last century and a half. Western man collectively is beginning to feel completely self-sufficient. In East Africa a dry year means starvation for the tribal families, a wet year means plenty and prosperity. They still feel the sense of being at the mercy of nature and the weather, and they respond with sacrifices of petition or gratitude, as the case may be. But in Birmingham, the news media may inform us that the whole strawberry crop in East Anglia is lost because of a dry spring, but it certainly does not mean life or death; in fact, it is not even much of an inconvenience— the consequences being no more than strawberries costing a few pence more. Our children do not die of diphtheria; they are not disfigured by smallpox; they do not have rickets. We trust modern medicine to protect us, and medicine is a human science. The majority of people in our Western culture optimistically assume that through science man can achieve mastery over the environment. No longer do we feel dependent on powers outside our control. This view is rather superficial, to the extent that we are in fact far more dependent on others for our essential supplies: we could not feed ourselves from our little town gardens, and our dependence on electricity is soon apparent when supplies are cut by industrial disputes. But still, we feel we are dependent on human rather than divine agencies to supply our wants.

This is not the place to enter into an elaborate dialogue

with the a-religiousness of our culture. Nevertheless, it does seem possible to suggest that there is a misplaced confidence in human success and man's ability to cope with his world. This optimism in fact puts enormous hidden strains on people, who feel they are expected to accomplish more and more, live at a faster and faster pace, and never fail to meet the demands made upon them. We may have subdued our physical environment in a way that man has never managed before, but it is extremely doubtful whether we are psychologically independent and self-sufficient. Most of us recoil from unfamiliar situations, and few can cope with crises without dependence on the support of others. There are, in fact, two sorts of dependence, a debilitating kind which saps individuality, and a recuperative kind, which contributes to the ability to function independently. Oscillation between dependence and independence is needed.

For the humanist, the answer to our need for support lies in the development of positive relationships between mature, integrated persons. Yet many of us only approximate to that integrity of personality in our best moments, and our relationships with others are usually far from perfect. As a child grows to maturity, he is only able to move to independence if he has security behind him, if he is able to depend on the accepting and supporting love of the mother, even when he rebels against that very dependence. For many people, independence is possible in maturity only because of a relationship of interdependence in marriage. Yet that very interdependence can cause strains. There is a tension between the need to be independent and the need to depend. No partner is, in any case, absolutely dependable; at some crucial moment, the idealized picture of the other person will not correspond with reality and the prop no longer serves its purpose. Total reliance cannot be placed on one who is not only human like yourself, but may even succumb to sickness or death. Human dependencies are inevitably transient. Dependence on God is alone utterly reliable; even when we try to assert our independence and go it alone, he provides the security which enables us to continue to function. A behavioural study[9] of church congregations has shown that 'going to Church, for most people, provides an opportunity to regress to dependence. This is a means of "re-creation", enabling them to operate with autonomy during the rest of the week'. The function of the Church in society, it was concluded, was to look after the dependency needs of people.

Some modern theologians like to speak of mankind coming of age and growing out of dependence on God. But psychology suggests that man's very independence and maturity depends on an underlying security and dependence. In expressing gratitude one is acknowledging that dependence. It is noticeable that the expression of genuine gratitude, the performance of acts of thanksgiving to others, gives a man a grace and dignity which otherwise he would not have. The man who takes everything for granted, who feels totally self-reliant, is neither attractive nor honest. Is this a clue to the fact that man was made to acknowledge his dependence and show thanksgiving in worship? Even if we find difficulty in thanking God for the washing-machine, the fruits of human ingenuity, even if we feel embarrassment at thanking God for sending rain to water the garden, which we regard as part of the natural process rather than a specific act of God, still we can at least acknowledge our dependence on his love for our ability to cope with the demands of our situation, and many find themselves going on to acknowledge their dependence on the Creator for their life and well-being. 'In him we live and move and have our being' (Acts 17.28).

So I want to suggest that the offering of sacrifices of praise and thanksgiving has been in the past a natural human response, and for many remains a central constituent in a religious response to life. There are moments for some of us when we desire to express our thanks to something beyond ourselves. It may not seem a very logical argument to claim that God must exist, because there must be someone to whom we can offer thanks, but it is sometimes an instinctive conviction. The churches were full at the end of the last war. People turned instinctively to traditional rituals to convey their relief and gratitude. To those who accept these instincts within themselves, to all who still respond to the world and to life in a religious way, sacrifices of praise and thanksgiving are as natural as they have ever been, though the means of expression may have changed through the influence of Christian spiritualizing, and sacrifice may no longer be the word we naturally employ for it. But we understand the joy that a mother feels in selfless service to her family: that sort of sacrificial living for others can be an expression of thanksgiving. Gratitude is usually expressed by saying 'thank-you' or offering a gift: the offering of prayer or gifts to charity, or gifts of time and effort in the service of others, these are means of expressing gratitude for us, just as they were for the early Church. We too have our symbols and rituals to express what sacrifice expressed in the ancient world.

In a Christian context, sacrifices of this kind are still part of the life of the Church, being worship offered to God, as creator and sustainer of all, and as redeemer of mankind. Because of the history we have been tracing, these acts of worship do not take the form of slaughtered animals, though the symbolism of the 'harvest-festival' lives on, and the offering of bread and wine in the eucharist is an offering of thanksgiving. Sacrifices of worship are offered through prayer, through offerings of love and charity, through personal dedication—not perhaps to die like the martyrs, but to live in imitation of Christ. Notice how closely the ideas of the early Christian Fathers are reflected in the

115

ideology of contemporary Christianity, though cultural conditions have made us see imitation of Christ more in terms of service to others, and less in terms of self-denial and withdrawal from the world. The worship and service of the Church are in the highest sense sacrificial; the word may have lost its full meaning, but the *fact* is part of the very life of the Church.

2

SACRIFICES OF COMMUNION

We found two types of communion-sacrifice: feasting *with* God, and feasting *on* God. The first of these clearly arose from the recognition that the good things provided by nature, or God, should not be enjoyed without sharing it with the divinity, or returning a token part to him. It implies some kind of kinship between God and ourselves. Table-fellowship was a bond of love.

Modern man is supposed to have grown out of the need to have any supernatural partner present in relationships. A relationship that is entirely satisfying can be found at the purely human level. Communion between people, social contact, is a human activity which always goes better over food and drink. The Methodists have a cup of tea, company directors a five-course dinner.

The religious view of life, however, remains true to the instinct of mankind that without reference to more ultimate values, it is all too easy for relationships to go wrong. The camaraderie can be exclusive and narrow; tensions can develop within it. It is within the most intimate of relationships that friction most easily arises, not in the superficial ones where politeness covers selfishness. To primitive man, sharing with gods or spirits was instinctive; it was the way to ensure survival. In *Lord of the Flies* we find the recognition that man has a beast inside himself which is more fearful than anything in his environment, a beast which causes disruption in relationships and the tragedy of man's inhumanity to man. Anthropologists and psychologists would speak rather of the animal instincts which are a natural part of human nature, not a foreign element. Yet even so, there is recognition that what is needed is a way of dealing with the disruptive emotions produced by our instincts. Self-interest and group-interests may have positive results, but, all too often, it is negative results that predominate: relationships break down through self-centredness and inability to understand another's point of view; communities fragment into hostile and prejudiced groups. For the early Christians, communion-sacrifice was a recognition of the fact that the presence of God in communion was needed to banish evil spirits, a recognition of the fact that community depends on communion with his spirit, the very principle of love. We may express it a little differently, but we surely need something of the same sort, a context in which the disruptive tendencies in personal relationships and society in general can find reconciliation. In Christian fellowship, and particularly in its most characteristic expression at the Table of the Lord, men seek community, a fellowship with each other and with God, in which our emotions can be sanctified and harnessed to positive ends.

The second type of communion-sacrifice depends on man's sense of inadequacy and need. Human beings are weak; they need the power of the gods. This they receive by consuming him. It was a perfectly natural analogy. Men keep up their strength by eating food; so if the power of the god resides in the superhuman energy of the bull, then this superhuman power can be assimilated by eating the bull's flesh.

Such a notion seems incredibly crude, and once more we find ourselves confronted by the common assumption of modern man that he needs no supernatural aid, however obtained. To accomplish great things, we do not practise magic or feed on 'God'; rather more rationally we go through an intensive training course or have a good night's sleep. But it may be that, in a sense, men need to feed on God as they have never needed it before, and the thing that distinguishes the religious man is his recognition of this fact. What tests the strength and courage of modern man is not great adventure or wild beasts or warring tribal neighbours. It is the attacks on his endurance made by the assembly line, by the noise and rush of city life, and by the endless, purposelessness of much of life as an industrial worker or housewife, or whatever forms the daily routine for each individual. When men lived closer to nature, this was not the pattern of their lives. There were periods, like the sowing and the harvest, when the work was desperately hard; there were times when the pressure was lifted. Tolstoy in *Anna Karenina* describes the peasants at harvest-time: 'all rancour and disharmony was swallowed up in the sea of cheerful common toil. God gave the day, God gave the strength for it. And the day and the strength were consecrated to labour, and that labour was its own reward.'[10] The modern world gives men greater opportunities. Life no longer is simply a struggle for survival. Yet at the same time it enslaves and cramps the vast majority. There is a need for superhuman resources to prevent ourselves being dehumanized, to save ourselves from losing the best of human values in the fume-polluted environment, and the rush for push-button enjoyment. We drive out of the city in our hoards to drink in fresh air and commune with nature. We seek means of creative expression in growing and arranging flowers. There seems to be a deep-seated instinct to seek the fulfilment of ourselves in a way that takes us beyond our personal limitations and the constrictions of our environment—beyond purely materialist ambitions to something of greater value and significance, even if it is no more than participating by proxy in the prowess of a great footballer or violinist.

In the Church we seek satisfaction above all in feeding on the body and blood of Christ in our hearts, and we find here a 'medicine of immortality',[11] something that sustains and fulfils us, something that gives value to life and carries us beyond our often petty day-to-day achievements and rewards. Communion-sacrifices, transformed by reinterpretation according to Christian ideas of fellowship with each other and with God, remain a central part of Christian life and worship.

3
SACRIFICES FOR SIN

Three types of sin-offering have been distinguished in our study; expiation, propitiation, and aversion. Sacrifices for sin arose out of the recognition that humanity has a problem, that something has gone wrong in the relationship between man and his environment, man and his fellow-man. Rites for dealing with guilt, sin, pollution, and defilement are a universal feature of human religious practices. Which type of sacrifice predominates in the religious thinking of a particular group depends on reactions to the problem of evil and sin; on how far man accepts responsibility for what has gone wrong, and how far he attributes it to powers outside himself; on how far man regards the universe as basically hostile and how far he regards it as basically favouring or loving.

1. *Expiation* means the removal of pollution, the cleansing of sin so that reconciliation can take place and relationships be restored. Something is done to wipe away the fault. Of course, in many cases it is quite impossible to restore the former position. If you are responsible for a road accident

in which a child is killed, you cannot expiate the fault by restoring that child to life. Expiation means an attempt to find substitute means of wiping away the fault, some method of covering the guilt, some symbol of release.

2. *Propitiation* implies a less profound acceptance of responsibility for the situation. It is an attempt to buy off the anger of the offended party. You are more conscious of the offence given than of your own guilt. You feel a need to appease. Sacrifices of propitiation arose from fear, from a sense of estrangement or alienation, the feeling that the universe is hostile because of sin. It is not all that long since a bad harvest was attributed to God's anger. Suffering is still thought of as a punishment. The driver of a minibus hired to transport some mentally handicapped children across Birmingham commented that the parents must have been very wicked to have children like that. For all our sophistication, such presuppositions survive among people today.

3. *Aversion* avoids admitting responsibility for evil or sin. You are not conscious of your own fault, so much as the fact that you could not help it. You are in the position of St Paul:

> It is no longer I that do it, but sin which dwells within me.... I can will what is right but I cannot do it. For I do not do the good I want, but the evil I do not want is what I do. If that is so, it is not I that do it, but sin which dwells within me (Rom. 7.18–20 RSV).

Paul is here expressing that sense of helplessness, of inability to do good, which many of us no doubt experience. It is not my fault I am irritable with the kids, it is because I am tired; it is not my fault I am possessive in my love for my family, it is part of my character; and nowadays, when family background or social deprivation explains and excuses delinquency, how much more are we tempted to make excuses for ourselves! Yet in our better moments we dislike our jealousy and selfishness. We feel we are in the grip of passions outside our control. We recognize in ourselves Paul's description of the divided personality: it is not me, but sin that does this. This is the modern equivalent to the more primitive belief in the power of evil spirits. Evil spirits, or sin, have to be driven from within us, by using some means of aversion. But it is not only sin which is a problem. Mankind has admitted his helplessness in the face of circumstances by attributing disease, war, famine, psychological disorders, poverty, hardship, and all manner of other mishaps to the activity of evil spirits. Sacrifices, men have felt, could keep away the evils that grip us, and free us from the sense of bondage and helplessness.

All sacrifices for sin are therefore concerned with the problem of evil in ourselves, and evil in our environment, and the three different types of sin-offering reflect different types of reaction to these problems. It is for this reason that the sacrifice of Christ has meant different things to different people. Let us look at each in turn in relation to the sin-offering made by Christ on the cross:

1. The predominant tendency in Western Christianity has been to think of it in terms of *propitiation*. Our cultural tradition has included a strong sense of the legal rights involved in a relationship, a sense of the balance of justice. So the natural reaction for many Christians in this context has been a deep awareness of the offence to God that sin has occasioned, and a primary concern with the need to make reparation. Yet, how could man make adequate reparation to God for the depth of his disobedience and sin? In this stream of tradition, atonement has naturally been understood as Christ offering reparation for us, Christ being punished on the cross instead of us, Christ bearing the consequences of God's just condemnation of our sin in our

place. This has always been a compelling image, and it is deeply engrained in our traditions of evangelism and faith. But surely we must recognize that it is inadequate if it is regarded as the *only* meaning of Christ's death, and also that its use as *explanation*, rather than *image* in conjunction with other images, has uncomfortable theological corollaries. Its problems and difficulties were explored in the last chapter. Yet, propitiation sacrifice has provided the key to the cross for many believers, and it remains psychologically forceful.

2. Down the centuries, the *aversion*-type of sacrifice has had widespread appeal to ordinary Christians as a means of understanding the sacrifice of Christ. We have explored Origen's use of the idea and seen that, in the last half-century, it has found a new lease of life. The death of Christ has been seen as the guarantee of God's ultimate victory over evil. The rediscovery of the old mythological picture of God's victory over the devil was made between the wars;[12] it has since been taken up and expounded by scholars who were extremely conscious of man's helplessness in the face of evils outside his own control, and made use of the familiar terminology of the 'occupation' and 'D-day'[13] to express their understanding of Christ's work. The experience of the Second World War gave them the sympathy needed to relive the beliefs of the ancient world in the powers of evil. For them, the gospel meant that there was no need to feel enslaved to these powers; rather we should take up arms in the struggle against evil, knowing that the battle has already been effectively won. The cross is a message of assurance that the world will not ultimately sink into a morass of evil chaos, and of hope that we can rise above the evil impulses which seem to grip us. The death of Christ was a sacrifice which overcame evil and rendered it ineffective. It was an aversion-sacrifice.

3. *Expiation*, as we have seen in the biblical term, and the understanding of Christ's sacrifice as an expiatory sacrifice have some very important emphases. Expiatory sacrifice is a means of wiping away the guilt, of dealing with the consciousness of the fault. Now animal sacrifice may not seem to be a very effective means in our eyes, but this is what was attempted, and in its aim it goes deeper than the more superficial attempts merely to get rid of the consequences of sin, namely anger and punishment. It should be psychologically more relevant. Furthermore, in the biblical tradition, expiation involved an emphasis on the fact that man is incapable of dealing with sin on his own account. God alone can remove the guilt, God alone can save from sin. The sacrifice of Christ is psychologically the most powerful enactment of all this. There we see God himself wiping away the guilt and the sin which have broken the relationship between him and his creatures. There we see God himself taking a truly costly way of suffering in order to make repentance possible, demonstrating his forgiveness so that sin no longer comes between us and him. Sin is so serious that forgiveness is no cheap, sentimental welcome-back. It involves God himself in the suffering and evil of his universe—in death itself.

Effective symbols do not have a single meaning. The symbols of art, music, literature, and religion convey different things to different people, even different things to the same person on different occasions. A good symbol is never exhausted by definitions or explanations; it appeals to the heart, not just the head. It is not therefore surprising to find these overlapping, even contradictory significances in the interpretation of Christ's sacrificial death. Basically these images have two areas of reference: (i) the problem of evil, pain and suffering, the illogical and inexplicable way in which life treats people, often we feel undeservedly; (ii) the problem of guilt and sin, the inner conflicts and weaknesses of human beings. Let us look at the relevance of Christ's sacrifice within each of these areas.

1. The problem of evil is the greatest difficulty faced by any developed religious philosophy. Possible conclusions include an ultimate dualism or a paradoxical monotheism, which is the way taken by Christian tradition. There have been many different attempts at theodicy, attempts to justify the ways of God to men. The world, as we experience it, is ambiguous; it sometimes appears good, it sometimes appears indifferent or hostile. The balance is not at all obviously on the side of those who believe in a good Creator and providential Father. But then the effect of evil and suffering is paradoxical; its existence and power call in question belief in God, and yet a religion of redemption from evil, like Christianity, requires its existence. The response of the religious man to life and to the universe depends on his feelings of inadequacy and dependence, feelings which are evoked by uncertainty, suffering, evil, the surd-element in life. Yet these are the very things which call in question his reliance on providence, the very things which produce intense religious doubts. There are mitigating philosophical answers to some forms of evil, like the suggestion that pain ennobles. But there are forms of suffering which seem utterly illogical in the scheme of things as conceived by those who believe in God and his purpose. How can we believe that God has created the world as a sort of school, to train characters fit for heaven, when two per cent of all human beings born are defective, so limited in their capacity that moral response is out of the question? When people face the reality of evil and suffering personally, philosophical answers are shown up as inadequate. The only answer is an absurdity, but an absurdity which appeals directly to age-long human instincts: the foolishness of the cross. If we look at the world around us, we do not see

many signs of God's sovereignty: mostly he is disregarded; often hostile forces seem more powerful; natural events and human actions seem outside his control, following their own patterns of cause and effect. But Christians respond in faith that the sacrifice of Christ on the cross is a guarantee that present appearances are not the ultimate. It is not just that God demonstrated his love to men. It is more than that; for God took upon himself the consequences of evil and sin. God accepted the terrible situation, demonstrating that he takes responsibility for evil in his universe, that he recognizes the seriousness of evil, its destructive effect, its opposition to his purposes; that it cannot be ignored, but must be challenged and removed; that it is costly to forgive; that he suffers because his universe is subject to evil and sin. Thus we see symbolically the sort of theoretical position reached in our discussion in the last chapter. In Steinbeck's novel, with which we began, we read the suggestive words:

> Christ nailed up might be more than a symbol of all pain. He might in very truth contain all pain. And a man standing on a hill-top with his arms outstretched, a symbol of a symbol, he too might be a reservoir of all the pain that ever was.[14]

2. It is inevitable that our discussion of how Christ's sacrifice deals with guilt and sin should have been partially anticipated in what was said earlier about the 'scapegoat' symbol. But let us spell out some of the assumptions made at that earlier stage.

It is sometimes said that modern man has no sense of sin. It is certainly true that some psychology encourages us to make excuses for ourselves, and to attribute our failings to our upbringing or circumstances. It is also true that the current 'humanism', contemporary confidence in man's self-sufficiency, leaves little room for man to go on his knees and weep tears of repentance to a power which he imagines is non-existent. But many now find it difficult whole-heartedly to subscribe to the 'official optimism'[15] which Western society expects of us. There are signs of dissatis-faction, signs of disquiet with a system which lives in the security of the H-bomb and condones massive injustices. It is a paradox that in this century in which two world wars have left guilt on the consciences of nations, there is a superficiality which admits no sin. In national and inter-national life, we find ourselves outraged by the inhuman tactics to which terrorists will resort for their own, often justifiable ends. We are quick to detect sin in others, and we blame them for it; circumstances may diminish responsi-bility, but in few cases do we allow that it absolves an offender entirely. If we are honest, we probably know sin in ourselves, also; as individuals we experience a sense of inadequacy, of inability to live as we know we ought in our relationships with other people, a sense of estrangement from others and frustration with ourselves. In his book on atonement, F. W. Dillistone suggests that a sense of *alienation* is the main feature common to modern literature and art-forms,[16] and the records of psychiatrists would seem to indicate that it is not only the artistically gifted who experience this. Indeed, if there is any consistent feature of depth psychology and modern anthropological theories, it is a recognition of the destructive side of human nature, the depths of violence, fear, anger, guilt and despair which we all try to suppress. As human beings, we inherit a tension between the instinct of self-preservation and the herd-instinct which will allow the community to take precedence over our own interests, a tension which produces personalities divided between love and hate, peace and aggression. An 'integrated personality' is able to cope with this tension, but most of us do so only inadequately.[17] This heredity produces, as our environment, a society of frustrated and alienated persons, estranged not only from each other but from themselves. How can such an analysis of the human situation refuse to acknowledge man's sin?

However, it is true that all too often we try to suppress our consciousness of it. In the respectability of modern society, we try to deny our aggressions, to escape from our guilt and inadequacy by pretending it is not there. There is an assumption around that we should all take a naturally optimistic and positive view of ourselves and of life, that we should all be considerate and selfless without effort, like those that William James called the 'once-born'.[18] But many of us know in our hearts that, if this is the front we put on, it is a façade. It covers inner struggles between concern for others and self-interest, between love and hate, between hope and despair. In the end our frustrations and resentments, our guilt and inadequacy, our inability to face ourselves or the demands made upon us by life, can no longer be suppressed and denied. Either they break out in fits of despair and irrational anger, or, as we saw in discussing the 'scapegoat', they are projected unconsciously on to others who seem to threaten our security. Insecurity breeds hostility. The cost is prejudice and terrorism in society, broken families, mental illness, perhaps even suicide, for individuals. It is true that most of us avoid such disasters, but the tendency is there. Wholeness and integrity can only be found by recognizing, accepting, and coping constructively with the aggressive and self-centred drives we possess.

So if we are realistic, we soon become conscious of human helplessness to create utopia; we are conscious, individually as well as by being members of society, of human failure to live up to ideals of love and justice to which the value-systems of our culture subscribe. In this context, the sacrifice of Christ is relevant, because it faces up to and accepts the situation. It shames us into climbing-down from our pillars of pride and self-sufficiency, into recognizing our inadequacy and the depths of our sin and guilt, into seeing our need for repentance; and having shamed us, it deals with the problem by offering acceptance, by offering unconditional forgiveness, by wiping away the guilt and alienation, by mending the estrangement. It can do this because in that sacrifice the tragic situation was unreservedly accepted and its terrible consequences drained to the dregs. The situation was not avoided or suppressed. The cup was not refused or passed on. Because he accepted it, we can know ourselves accepted in spite of consciousness of guilt, in spite of being unacceptable.

We need to reawaken this symbolical significance of the tragic death of Christ as the symbolical and ritual way of dealing with guilt and sin, and offering liberation. Sometimes a new presentation helps us to feel its power again. The musical *Godspell* dresses up the old language in a lively and powerful contemporary presentation, Christ dying for playing at life instead of seriously getting down to business, for flouting conventional securities and the materialistic aims of society, for being free and therefore rousing the hostility of those enmeshed in society's rat-race. His sacrifice for freedom is the means of our liberation. A similar theme is presented in a very different cultural setting by Nikos Kazantzakis in his novel, *Christ Recrucified* (or *The Greek Passion*).[19] A band of refugee Greeks arrive at a Greek village in Turkey, uprooted for insurrection by the forces of the Turkish army. The rich and comfortable village of Lycovrissi is jealous of its possessions and security. The outsiders are a dangerous threat to society, upheld by religion, country, honour, and private property. The villagers end by becoming in league with the Turkish authorities to drive out the starving refugees, the 'bolsheviks'—but not before one of their own number, Manolios, had tried to show them what the teaching of Christ meant in circumstances like that. At the beginning of the novel, Manolios had been chosen by the village

128

council to act the part of Christ in the mystery-play next Easter, but by Christmas the village has lynched him for identifying with the refugees and assisting them to take violent possession of lands and goods given them by one of his followers, the son of the village archon, who had been chosen to play the Apostle John. Manolios became the focus of the hostility of the village and the victim of the villagers' rage at the disruptions caused by the actions and attitudes he inspired in his associates. The power of the novel lies in the fact that those chosen to act parts in the passion-play live out in a subtle manner the characters for which they were chosen. In the final scene, the local priest unconsciously plays the part of Caiaphas, and the Turkish Agha that of Pilate, conspiring to get rid of Manolios, the disrupter of society. Manolios becomes the 'scapegoat', but he is not merely excommunicated; he is slain, and his sacrifice was made willingly to give the opportunity of new life to the refugee people. 'Dear Manolios', reflects the refugees' priest at the end of the novel, 'they've killed you for taking our sins upon you; you cried: "It was I who robbed, it was I who killed, and set things on fire; I nobody else!" so that they might let the rest of us take root peacefully in these lands ... In vain, Manolios, in vain will you have sacrificed yourself ...' He listened to the bell pealing gaily, announcing that Christ was coming down to earth to save the world.... He shook his head and heaved a sigh. 'In vain, my Christ, in vain,' he muttered; 'two thousand years have gone by and men crucify you still. When will you be born, my Christ, and not be crucified any more, but live among us for eternity?' The novel ends with this note of despair.

Yet the telling of the story is not in vain:

Each went down into the recesses of himself, saw his own soul and shivered. What murders, what infamies, what acts of shame there are boiling in the depths of us! We stay good because we are afraid. Our desires remain hidden, unslaked, furious; they poison our blood. But we contain ourselves, deceive our neighbours, and die honoured and virtuous. In the light of day we have done no evil all our life. But there is no deceiving God.[20]

The words of the novel express its total effect, as we see respectable people like ourselves revealed for what they are. And Manolios' sacrifice is only in vain if its immediate results are reckoned. Maybe the refugees had to take to the road again, but nevertheless it was a triumph of love and self-giving, a potent appeal, a sign of hope, a symbol that man is not wholly mean, cowardly, and self-interested. The cup was not refused, but drunk to the dregs. The horrors of human nature were recognized and their consequences voluntarily accepted. The martyr by his sacrifice can expiate the sin of the people. We respond to his sacrifice because sacrificial death is deeply rooted in the human mind, a constantly recurring theme of religion and folklore, myth and legend. As 'scapegoat' or sacrifice, an innocent victim can bear our sin. We may not be able to rationalize the effectiveness of the symbol, but it appeals to the imagination as poetic truth.

The same is true of the death of Christ. In some strange way the human response to Christ's sacrificial death is instinctive.

Traditional and conventional images of sacrifice may have been outmoded [writes Dillistone]. In some mysterious way, the Man upon the Cross retains his place in the human imagination as the timeless symbol of reconciliation through sacrifice.[21]

In art, music and literature, he is unlikely to lose it completely. As Paul said, it is a stumbling-block to the Jews (who may be understood as people who demand clear evidence); it is foolishness to the Greeks (who stand for intellectuals who demand purely rational solutions to philosophical problems), but to those who respond to the symbol, to those who sense its truth, the cross is the power of God and the wisdom of God. Age-old religious instincts enable us to make that response, whether we can explain it or not.

7

God and sacrificial worship

In the last two chapters, we have been asking whether our historical study has any consequences for theology and the Church today. In doing so, we have recognized the bankruptcy of calls to go 'back to the Bible' or 'back to the early Church'. The world has moved on and the cultural environment has changed much. Our intention has certainly *not* been to try to re-establish the doctrinal position reached in our historical study. Rather we have been asking whether on looking back in this way, we can discern things that are relevant to our situation; whether there are lost ideas which might enrich our understanding; whether there are valid analogies between their situation and ours.

There is one area in which our situation is exactly parallel to theirs. The Church in every age has to wrestle with the problem of presenting the gospel in terms relevant to the contemporary world, while at the same time preserving the distinctiveness of its message. How far should the Church be prepared to draw on the present cultural environment and how far should it deliberately refuse to compromise the classic and traditional expressions of its faith and worship?

For the early Church, the symbolic use of sacrifice language tended in both directions: it served the purpose of interpreting the gospel and the life of the Church in terms readily understood in the contemporary world, while at the same time maintaining the distinctiveness of its position over against other cults and philosophies. Our historical study suggests that, if Christianity is to be true to itself, it must have elements of exclusiveness, elements of refusal to compromise with its cultural environment, while at the same time changing to meet the contemporary situation. Unrestrained syncretism, that is, compromise with every current idea and practice so as to lose distinctiveness, was a path firmly rejected by the early Church—so firmly that martyrs lost their lives for their faith. Yet at the same time Christian thinkers adopted the thought-forms of their contemporaries and presented the gospel in the language and symbols with which they were familiar. Always there were groups which were prepared to go too far in one direction or the other, the exclusivist versus the liberal; but the mainstream of Christian tradition oscillated around the middle path.

It seems to me that the perennial task of theology lies precisely here—in finding a way of presenting the Christian gospel in terms that are relevant in the cultural environment of the time or location, while remaining true to the essential and distinctive traditions of the faith. These are the criteria by which theology must be measured—by its success or failure to meet these requirements. Neither conservatism nor radicalism alone can do justice to the required balance of extremes.

Contemporary theology bears, as it should, the marks of cultural conditioning. There are repeated attempts to wrest the gospel out of its traditional mould, each meeting with response or reaction from the faithful. How should we appraise these attempts? The early Church refused to compromise with idolatry because of a deep-seated instinct that it meant disloyalty to their God. I suspect that we have to refuse to compromise with a complete 'secularizing' of religion, with attempts to satisfy fundamental religious drives in other ways. The rejection of sacrificial imagery is to be linked with the tendency to reject traditional modes of devotion and prayer. It reflects an uneasiness with the traditional picture of God in the face of scientific humanism. Some of this uneasiness is certainly justified, but I suspect that the Church needs to set its face against many of these reductionist attempts, even though they come in Christian dress and seek to uphold Christian values. Theology has always recognized the poverty of our pictures of God, but that does not mean that traditional images are false. They need to be deepened and freed from traditional strait-jackets. We need a new appreciation of the layers of meaning in religious symbols, to rediscover the power of instinctive symbols that still find expression in art and likewise, to see these as a valid way of talking about worship and present-ing the gospel today. The balance between traditional and contemporary modes of expression needs to be maintained, especially in the context of worship.

Sacrifice is surely one of the symbols to which these observations apply. It is not only a symbol of long-standing and deep significance in the Christian tradition, but also, I suggest, not so foreign to our time as many have supposed. In the last chapter, the aim was to show that modern studies of the nature of man suggest that sacrificial symbol-ism is basic to man's make-up and can still meet with response. What we need to do is to make the symbolism live again, released from cramping and deadening definitions which have killed it. We explored examples of how novels and drama may help us to do this and may enable us to rediscover the importance of sacrificial imagery.

Yet there is a danger in uncritical use of this symbolism. In Chapter 6, we subjected traditional interpretations of the symbols to examination, and suggested that they had been impoverished by narrow and inadequate assumptions about their meaning. A new use of the symbolism is likewise open to false and inadequate interpretations. It would be easy to treat some of the things said in the last chapter as pure fantasy, a myth of a dying and rising god, emotively satisfying but not in fact corresponding to any sort of reality. Many of our contemporaries appreciate Bach's St Matthew Passion as an aesthetic and even cathartic experience, but have no religious belief. It would be easy to allow some of the suggestions made to sink to the level of pure superstition. I am told that in Lancashire a mother still cannot go out after the birth of a baby until she has been 'churched'. Many parents with no church connections feel that baptism for their children is a necessity. It may be that the Church should not be too impatient of these superstitious survivals, since the compulsion probably stems from a deep-seated human need for ritual in relation to the major transitions of life: birth, marriage, death. Nor should we underestimate the salutary effect of secular performances of drama and music of religious origin. Yet one cannot help feeling that these examples fall far short of the Christian understanding of sacrifice and sacrament. We need some sort of rational critique of the symbols to purify them of false meanings.

What is to be the basis of this critique? The answer to this question is already implicit in our discussions. In our historical study, we found that the concept of sacrifice was intimately related to the concept of the divine. Once people realized that it was unworthy of God's majesty and self-sufficiency to think that he was dependent on sacrifice for food or pleasure, such an understanding of sacrifice became unacceptable. Ultimately our use of sacrificial symbols must be tested against the Christian understanding of God. The same basic point underlay our discussion of atonement in Chapter 6. Theories of atonement stand or fall by the concept of God implicit in them, and if their expression is at variance with the nature of the God and Father of our Lord Jesus Christ, they must be rejected.

Our understanding of sacrifice, therefore, must be informed by our understanding of the nature of God as revealed in Jesus Christ. Intimately related to this is our understanding of prayer, since prayer and sacrifice are in the end indistinguishable when it comes to a consideration of their purpose and rationale. Our concept of God should inevitably rule out inadequate conceptions of prayer, sacrifice and worship. What sort of a God is it who is so transcendent that our needs and responses have no relevance to him? Conversely, what sort of a God is it who likes to be told how marvellous he is and changes his mind in our favour if we give him the promise of a good offering in return?

If there is anything implicit in our exposition of sacrificial symbolism within Christian tradition, it is surely a warning against an oversimplified picture of God as harsh judge or indulgent Father. The God to whom we offer sacrifice is a God who first offered a sacrifice himself. The God to whom we cry in trouble is a God who took upon himself the cry of suffering humanity: My God, my God, why hast thou forsaken me? The God to whom we pray is not one who lightly changes his mind over trivial matters, but the God who bears the cost of conflict in his creation; a God who is transcendent but also immanent; a God who is involved in the pain, the suffering, the guilt, and the sin of his world; a God who allows us to share in his sacrifice for the salvation of his people. That is why he can rejoice in our sacrifices of praise and thanksgiving, and hearken to the petitions offered before his cross. Sacrificial worship is the only adequate and worthy response to the sacrifice of God. Awareness of this will prevent our responses from being merely emotional or superstitious. The factuality of the cross demands a response of total commitment.

In Christian tradition, the different types of sacrifice and the psychological needs they fulfilled are all found in a spiritualized form. Sacrifice is integral to a religious outlook. The Christian spiritual cult is a complete and total one, embracing in its symbols the reactions and instincts of many types of men. In this Christian spiritual cult, the sacrifice of Christ has always had a central and focal position. It was the sacrifice by which God reconciled the world to himself, the sacrifice in which he took responsibility for evil, accepted us as we are, and accepted into himself the consequences of evil and sin. Such an understanding of Christ's sacrifice transforms the sacrifices offered by Christians; for in the light of his death, men recognize the inadequacy of their attempts to justify themselves, or expiate their own sin. All a man can do is to respond with repentance to the all-sufficient sacrifice of Christ. Sacrifice is not simply giving up but receiving and offering in response. Thus, the believer is drawn into the sacrifice of Christ, called to engage with him in the war against evil, sin and suffering, called to purify himself by response to his sacrificial blood, and called to bear the sufferings of others by sacrificial living. Thus Christian sin-offerings are transformed by their relationship with the sacrifice of Christ. Sacrifices of worship and thanksgiving are likewise focused on this central sacrificial act; for worship is offered not simply for creation and preservation and all the good things of life, but chiefly for that costly act of forgiveness and reconciliation. Above all, the sacrifice of communion is transformed. The central act of sacrifice performed by Christians is a fellowship-meal, through which believers share in the redemptive sacrifice of Christ by commemoration, a symbolic meal shared in his presence with fellow-believers, a meal in which the actions of breaking bread and drinking wine enable us to feed spiritually on his 'virtue' and vitality. In fact, all types of sacrifice are summed up here. The eucharist is a sacrifice of worship, praise and thanksgiving, in which we offer a gift-sacrifice, the first-fruits of bread and wine, the substance of life. The eucharist is a sacrifice for sin, in which the representation in sacramental form of the sin-offering made by Christ realizes in us God's act of atonement. In fact, the early Church even thought of it as an aversion-sacrifice, believing that sharing in the feast kept away the devil and his angels; indeed, in whatever sense the sacrifice of Christ is understood, so is the sacrifice of the eucharist, and thus it is a sacrifice with the power to deal with sin and guilt and reconcile us with God. But primarily, it is a communion-sacrifice which draws us into fellowship with him and with each other, a meal in which we partake of his power and receive the strength to continue the battle against evil and sin within ourselves and in the world around us.

The place of Christ's continuing sacrificial work is in the sacrificial worship and sacrificial living of the Christian community, and in involvement like his in the sufferings of his world.

Thus in the concept of sacrifice are enshrined the deepest experiences of the Christian religion and the most far-reaching challenges, both to the individual believer and to the Church as a community. It covers the basic gospel of forgiveness in Christ, and its outworking in worship and service. Can any other image or symbol claim so much? We have had a long journey of re-discovery to bring alive the language of sacrifice, but there is a sense in which the reality of it will never be lost as long as there are people who find value and meaning in life through 'looking unto Jesus'.

Notes

Publication details are only given for those books which do not appear in the Bibliography on pp. 3-4.

INTRODUCTION

1. F. W. Dillistone, *The Christian Understanding of Atonement*, and F. R. Barry, *The Atonement*.

2. The phrases quoted in this paragraph are taken from T. J. J. Altizer and William Hamilton, *Radical Theology and the Death of God* (Indianapolis 1966).

3. Originally published in Britain by Heinemann, 1935; Corgi editions from 1958.

4. First published by Faber and Faber, 1954; published in Penguin books since 1960.

CHAPTER 1

1. Augustine, *De Civitate Dei* x.6.

2. For details and examples, see W. D. Rouse, *Greek Votive Offerings* (Cambridge 1902).

3. Xenophon, *Anabasis* iii.2.12.

4. 'Negotium', by H. Schmidt, *Veteres philosophi quomodo iudicaverint de precibus* (Giessen 1908).

5. Origen, *Exhortation to Martyrdom* 45. Cf. also *Contra Celsum* iii.28ff, etc. Earlier the same idea is found in Athenagoras, *Legatio pro Christianis*, 26-7.

6. J. E. Harrison, *Prolegomena to the Study of Greek Religion* (3rd edn, Cambridge 1922). Since Harrison's work, this aspect of Greek religion has been generally recognized in books on the subject.

7. E.g., Amos 4 and 5.

8. Enoch 9.6; 10.4-8.

9. It is important to be clear about the distinction made here between propitiatory and expiatory sacrifices. The English words have been used loosely and interchangeably, but this distinction has become current in the relevant theological literature of modern scholarship.

CHAPTER 2

1. E.g., Deut. 6.21; 26.5.

2. E.g., Amos 4 and 5; Micah 6.6-8; Isaiah 1.10-17; etc.

3. For discussion of this question, see: C. J. Lindblom, *Prophecy in*

Ancient Israel (Oxford, 1962); H. Wheeler Robinson, *Inspiration and Revelation in the Old Testament* (Oxford, 1946); N. W. Porteous' essay in *Record and Revelation* (ed. H. W. Robinson, Oxford 1938); etc.

4. For the place of the Psalms in worship, see S. O. P. Mowinckel, *The Psalms in Israel's Worship* (ET by D. Ap-Thomas, Oxford 1962).

5. Four Psalms almost reach the level of condemnation of sacrifice, 40, 50, 51 and 69.

6. Pss. 1, 15, 24, 119, etc.

7. C. G. Montefiore and H. Loewe, *A Rabbinic Anthology* (London 1938), pp. 430–431.

8. E.g., Josephus, *Contra Apionem* ii.192; and Philo, see below, note 21.

9. Quotations from the Dead Sea Scrolls are taken from G. Vermes, *The Dead Sea Scrolls in English* (Pelican 1962), pp. 87–90; 101–113; 240.

10. *On Sacrifices* i and ix.

11. Xenophon, *Memorabilia* i.3; Plato, *Phaedrus* 279 B.C.

12. E.g., Persius, *Satire* 2; Maximus of Tyre, *Dissertationes* xi (On Prayer).

13. Maximus, *op. cit.*

14. E.g., Cicero, *De Natura Deorum* i.4, 14, 77.

15. Maximus, op. cit.; Marcus Aurelius, *Meditations*.

16. His *De Abstinentia* ii is the source for Porphyry's various arguments.

17. Justin, *I Apology* xiii.

18. *Stromateis* vii, 14, 15, 31, 33.

19. *Epistle to Anebo* 4, 5.

20. Iamblichus' discussion is found in *De Mysteriis* v.

21. For the various points made, see: *De Spec. Leg.* I. 257, 167, etc.; *Sac.* 84; *Plant.* 108, 126; *Deus* 7–8; *Det.* 20–21.

22. *Corpus Hermeticum* i.31; xii.23; xiii.18, 21; *Asclepius* 41.

CHAPTER 3

1. *Barnabas* xvi.

2. Origen, *Contra Celsum* i.69; iii.81; vii.44ff.; viii.17ff.; etc.

3. *Hermas* iii.7.

4. E.g., *Barnabas* ii.7–8; Irenaeus, *Adversus Haereses* iv.17.1–4; Origen, *Homilies on Leviticus* ii.5; iv.5; etc.

5. E.g., Justin, *Dialogue with Trypho* 117.

6. E.g., *I Clement* xviii, lii.

7. *Barnabas* ii.10; Clement, *Paedagogus* iii.90.

8. For discussion of the evidence, see W. H. C. Frend, *Martyrdom and Persecution in the Early Church* (Oxford 1965).

9. Origen, *Exhortation* 22–27; Gregory Nazianzen, *Oration* xv.

10. For the various points made, see *Romans* iv.2, vi.3; *Ephesians* xxi.1; *Smyrnaeans* x.2; *Polycarp* ii.3, vi.1.

11. Origen, *Contra Celsum* vi.70; vii.44.

12. Aristides i; Justin, *I Apology* **x**, xiii; Clement, *Stromateis* vii.14, 15; Irenaeus, *Adversus Haereses* iv. 14, 17, 18; Origen, *Contra Celsum* viii.62.
13. *Stromateis* vii.15.
14. Ibid. vii. 14, 31, 33.
15. *De Civitate Dei* xix.23.
16. Origen, *Homilies on Leviticus* ix.9.
17. *Didache* xiii; cf. Hippolytus, *Apostolic Tradition* **xxviii** (ed. Dix).
18. Irenaeus, *Adversus Haereses* iv.17.5.
19. Hippolytus, op. cit. iii.

CHAPTER 4

1. C. H. Dodd, *The Apostolic Preaching and its Development* (London 1936).
2. Pseudo-Chrysostom (usually attributed to Hippolytus): ed. P. Nautin, *Trois Homélies dans la tradition d'Origène* (Sources Chrétiennes).
3. Gregory Nazianzen, *Oration* i.
4. *Homilies on Hebrews* xvi and xxix.
5. Ibid. xxv.
6. Ibid. xxix.
7. *Contra Celsum* iv.72 (trans. H. Chadwick).
8. *Homilies on Jeremiah* xviii.6.
9. Origen argues this himself in his *Commentary on Romans* ii.1, iii.1.
10. *Homilies on Leviticus* vii.2, v.4; *Commentary on John* i.38.
11. *Homilies on Leviticus* iii.1,
12. *Commentary on Romans* vi.12.
13. *Homilies on Leviticus* v.3.
14. See G. Aulén, *Christus Victor.*
15. *Commentary on John* ii.4, 21.
16. Ibid. vi.35.
17. *Contra Celsum* i.31; cf. *Commentary on John* vi.36.
18. *Commentary on Romans* iv.11.
19. *Contra Arianos* ii.7ff.
20. *Homilies on Leviticus* ii.3.

CHAPTER 5

1. E.g., J. Rivière, *The Doctrine of Atonement* (ET by L. Cappadelta, London 1909); James Denney, *The Christian Doctrine of Reconciliation* (London 1917).
2. H. Rashdall, *The Idea of Atonement in Christian Theology* (London 1919).
3. Further discussion will be found in my paper, 'Insight or incoherence? The Greek Fathers on God and Evil' in J. E. H. **xxiv** pp. 113–26 (1973).

4. C. F. D. Moule, *The Sacrifice of Christ*, p. 28.

CHAPTER 6

1. Anthony Storr, *Jung* (Fontana 1973), pp. 112–13. Cf. Mircea Eliade, *Images and Symbols* (ET by Philip Mairet, London 1961); and Victor White, *God and the Unconscious*.

2. Augustine, *De Civitate Dei* x.6.

3. Especially his trilogy, *The Lord of the Rings* (London 1954).

4. Anthony Storr, op. cit.

5. Jeremy Burnham, *Judas Goat*, shown on 22 March 1973.

6. For these comments on 'scapegoating', I am particularly indebted to discussions with Michael Wilson and his group of Pastoral Studies students at the University of Birmingham.

7. See further, Henry McKeating, *Living with Guilt*, ch. 5.

8. See further, Anthony Storr, *The Integrity of the Personality*.

9. Bruce Reed, *Going to Church* (Explorations in the Study of Human Behaviour, 2), published by the Grubb Institute of Behavioural Studies (1970).

10. ET by Rosemary Edmonds (Penguin Classics 1954), p. 297.

11. Ignatius, *Ephesians* xx.

12. G. Aulén, op. cit.

13. See further, F. W. Dillistone, op. cit. p. 105ff.

14. Corgi edition, p. 68.

15. A phrase used in an unpublished paper by J. Moltmann, *The Crucified God*, prepared for the conference of the Society for the Study of Theology, April 1973. By coincidence, some of the views expressed here are found differently expressed in that paper.

16. Dillistone, op. cit. chs 1 and 10.

17. See further, Anthony Storr, *The Integrity of the Personality*; H. A. Williams, *The True Wilderness*; Henry McKeating, op. cit.

18. *The Varieties of Religious Experience* (Gifford Lectures 1901–2).

19. ET by Jonathan Griffin, Oxford 1954; Faber Paperback editions since 1962. American Editions under the title, *The Greek Passion*.

20. Faber edn, p. 184.

21. Op. cit. p. 399.

Bibliography

For further reading:

Pagan Religion

G. Murray, *Five Stages of Greek Religion* (Oxford 1925).

H. J. Rose, *Ancient Greek Religion* (London 1948).
— , *Ancient Roman Religion* (London 1949).

E. R. Dodds, *The Greeks and the Irrational* (Berkeley 1951).

Old Testament

G. B. Gray, *Sacrifice in the Old Testament* (Oxford 1925).

H. H. Rowley, 'The Meaning of Sacrifice in the Old Testament' (article republished in *From Moses to Qumran*, London 1964).

R. de Vaux, *Ancient Israel*: Vol. 2, Religious Institutions; ET by John McHugh (London 1961).

H. Ringgren, *Sacrifice in the Bible* (London 1962).

Background to the rise of Christianity

R. K. Yerkes, *Sacrifice in Greek and Roman Religion and in early Judaism* (London 1953).

T. R. Glover, *The Conflict of Religions in the early Roman Empire* (London 1909).

A. D. Nock, *Conversion* (Oxford 1933).

Christian Doctrine

V. Taylor, *Jesus and his Sacrifice* (London 1959).

H. E. W. Turner, *The Patristic Doctrine of Redemption* (London 1952).

G. Aulén, *Christus Victor* (ET by A. G. Hebert, London 1931).

SACRIFICE AND THE DEATH OF CHRIST

C. F. D. Moule, *The Sacrifice of Christ* (London 1956).

H. A. Hodges, *The Pattern of Atonement* (London 1963).

F. W. Dillistone, *The Christian Understanding of Atonement* (London 1968).

F. R. Barry, *The Atonement* (London 1968).

Other literature

Victor White, O.P., *God and the Unconscious* (London 1952).

Anthony Storr, *The Integrity of the Personality* (Penguin 1960).

H. A. Williams, *The True Wilderness* (Penguin 1965).

Kenneth Slack, *Is Sacrifice Outmoded?* (London 1966).

Henry McKeating, *Living with Guilt* (London 1970).

Index of Names and Subjects

Index of Biblical References

SACRIFICE AND THE DEATH OF CHRIST